Answer Key

Family and Community

Fourth Edition

Note: The fact that materials produced by other publishers may be referred to in this volume does not constitute an endorsement of the content or theological position of materials produced by such publishers. Any references and ancillary materials are listed as an aid to the student or the teacher and in an attempt to maintain the accepted academic standards of the publishing industry.

FAMILY AND COMMUNITY Student Activities Answer Key
Fourth Edition
Heritage Studies 1

Coordinating Writer
Jill Blackstock, MEd

Writer
Carol Arrington Ardt, MEd

Consultant
L. Michelle Rosier

Biblical Worldview
Brian C. Collins, PhD
Bryan Smith, PhD

Academic Oversight
Jeff Heath, EdD
Rachel Santopietro, MEd

Editor
Suzanne Villegas, MA

Designer
Garison Plourde

Concept Designers
Michael Asire
Julianne Bixler

Page Layout
Sarah Centers

Illustrators
Paula Cheadle
Cynthia Long
Sandy Mehus
Ambrose Rouse
Dana Thompson
Courtney Wise
Pixel Mouse House

Permissions
Sharon Belknap
Tatiana Bento
Elizabeth Walker

Project Coordinator
Heather Chisholm

Photo Credits
Key: (t) top; (c) center; (b) bottom; (l) left; (r) right

11t LUKASZ-NOWAK1/iStock/Getty Images Plus/Getty Images; 11tc © iStock.com/NicolasMcComber; 11bc JenniferPhotographyImaging/E+/Getty Images; 11b Artazum/Shutterstock.com; 21l Found Image Holdings Inc /Corbis Historical/Getty Images; 21r Weekend Images Inc./iStock / Getty Images Plus/Getty Images; 35 Robert Nicholas/OJO Images/Getty Images; 41 Caia Images|Robert Daly/Media Bakery; 52tl HRAUN/E+/Getty Images; 52tr FatCamera/E+/Getty Images; 52cl Design Pics/Design Pics RF/Getty Images; 52cr Tetra images/Getty Images; 52bl Ariel Skelley/DigitalVision /Getty Images; 52br Hill Street Studios/DigitalVision/Getty Images; 57 (school) Ariel Skelley/Photodisc/Getty Images; 57 (Christmas) SolStock/E+ /Getty Images; 57 (meal) Adobe Stock/Monkey Business; 57 (hug) fizkes /iStock/Getty Images Plus/Getty Images; 57 (church) © iStock.com /FatCamera; 57 (police) © iStock.com/aijohn784; 65tl andresr/E+/Getty Images; 65tr Hispanolistic/E+/Getty Images; 65bl Bob Thomas/DigitalVision /Getty Images; 65br John Roman Images/Shutterstock.com; 67tl Monty Rakusen/Cultura/Getty Images; 67tr Adobe Stock/WavebreakmediaMicro; 67cl zeremski/iStock/Getty Images Plus/Getty Images; 67cr PeopleImages /E+/Getty Images; 67bl PhotoTalk/E+/Getty Images; 67br Adobe Stock/sima; 73t Maskot/Getty Images; 73ct Jose Luis Pelaez Inc/DigitalVision/Getty Images; 73cc avid_creative/E+/Getty Images; 73cb Adobe Stock/Monkey Business; 73b Jose Luis Pelaez Inc/DigitalVision/Getty Images; 109 Bettmann/Getty Images; 113 (1 year) Oksana Kuzmina/Shutterstock.com; 113 (3 years) Juanmonino/E+/Getty Images; 113 (4 years) Jonathan Novack /Shutterstock.com; 113 (5 years) Rob Hainer/Shutterstock.com; 125bg "Seal of the President of the United States"/Wikimedia Commons/Public Domain; 131tl Age Fotostock/Emilio Ferrer/Media Bakery; 131tr Baimieng /Shutterstock.com; 131bl Andrey Mertsalov/Shutterstock.com; 131br catnap72/E+/Getty Images; 135t Adobe Stock/Alexandr Mitiuc; 135c Hulton Deutsch/Corbis Historical/Getty Images; 135b typhoonski/iStock Editorial /Getty Images Plus/Getty Images; 137t "Brooklyn Bridge New York City 1899 Pedestrian Crossing"/Library of Congress/Wikimedia Commons /Public Domain; 137b "Large-scale-old-map-of-the-united-states-the-british-provinces-and-mexico-1849"/J.M. Atwood/Wikimedia Commons /Public Domain; 139tl Metropolitan Art Museum, New York, Gift of Charles and Valerie Diker, 1999, www.metmuseum.org; 139tr RASimon/iStock/Getty Images Plus/Getty Images; 139cl Adobe Stock/boonchuay1970; 139cr Water Jar, Zuni Pueblo, c.1880 (earthenware), American / Museum of Fine Arts, Boston, Massachusetts, USA / Everett Fund / Bridgeman Images; 139bl LisaValder/E+/Getty Images; 139br Covered basket container, c.1875 (porcupine quills & birch bark), Native American / Museum of Fine Arts, Boston, Massachusetts, USA / Gift of Mr. and Mrs. William White Howells / Bridgeman Images; 145l "Constitution of the United States, page 1" /Wikimedia Commons/Public Domain; 145r "United States Declaration of Independence"/Wikimedia Commons/Public Domain; 147t Adobe Stock /Paul Wossidlo; 147ct SPUTNIK / Alamy Stock Photo; 147cc © iStock.com /zokru; 147cb MSPhotographic/Shutterstock.com; 147b bhofack2/iStock /Getty Images Plus/Getty Images; 148t © iStock.com/Gannet77; 148ct mphillips007/iStock/Getty Images Plus/Getty Images; 148cc Pixelchrome Inc/DigitalVision/Getty Images; 148cb rez-art/iStock/Getty Images Plus /Getty Images; 148b Stephen Barnes/Ireland/Alamy Stock Photo; 153t "Constitution of the United States, page 1"/Wikimedia Commons/Public Domain; 153b "United States Declaration of Independence"/Wikimedia Commons/Public Domain

Maps from Map Resources

Originally published as *HERITAGE STUDIES 1 Activity Manual Answer Key*.

Creation

Draw pictures to answer the questions. Color the picture.

1. What is one thing God made to be in the sky?

2. What is one thing God made to be in the water?

3. What is one thing God made to be on the land?

4. What people were part of the first family?

The Fall and Redemption

Mark an *X* on each picture that shows a result of the Fall.

1.
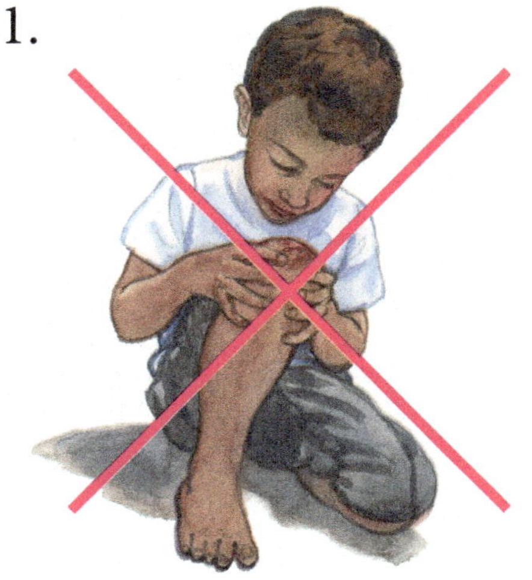

2.

3.

4.

Mark the word that completes the sentence.

5. Jesus died on a cross to pay for _____.

　○ redemption　　　● sin

6. Jesus' payment is called _____.

　● redemption　　　○ sin

Family Roles

Draw a line from the role to the correct family member.

1. leads the family

2. helps the husband

3. obey their parents

4. leads the children

5. learn how to live

God has given you the role of a child in your family.
Draw a smiley face 😊 for each job you have done well this week.

○ 6. I put my toys away.

○ 7. I obeyed right away.

○ 8. I obeyed cheerfully.

○ 9. I finished my schoolwork.

○ 10. I did chores to help my family.

My Bedroom

Name ___________________________

My Bedroom

Cut out the pictures to make a map of your bedroom.

Family and Community

Types of Homes

Draw a line from the home to the place where you might find it.
Circle the word that best describes the place where you live.

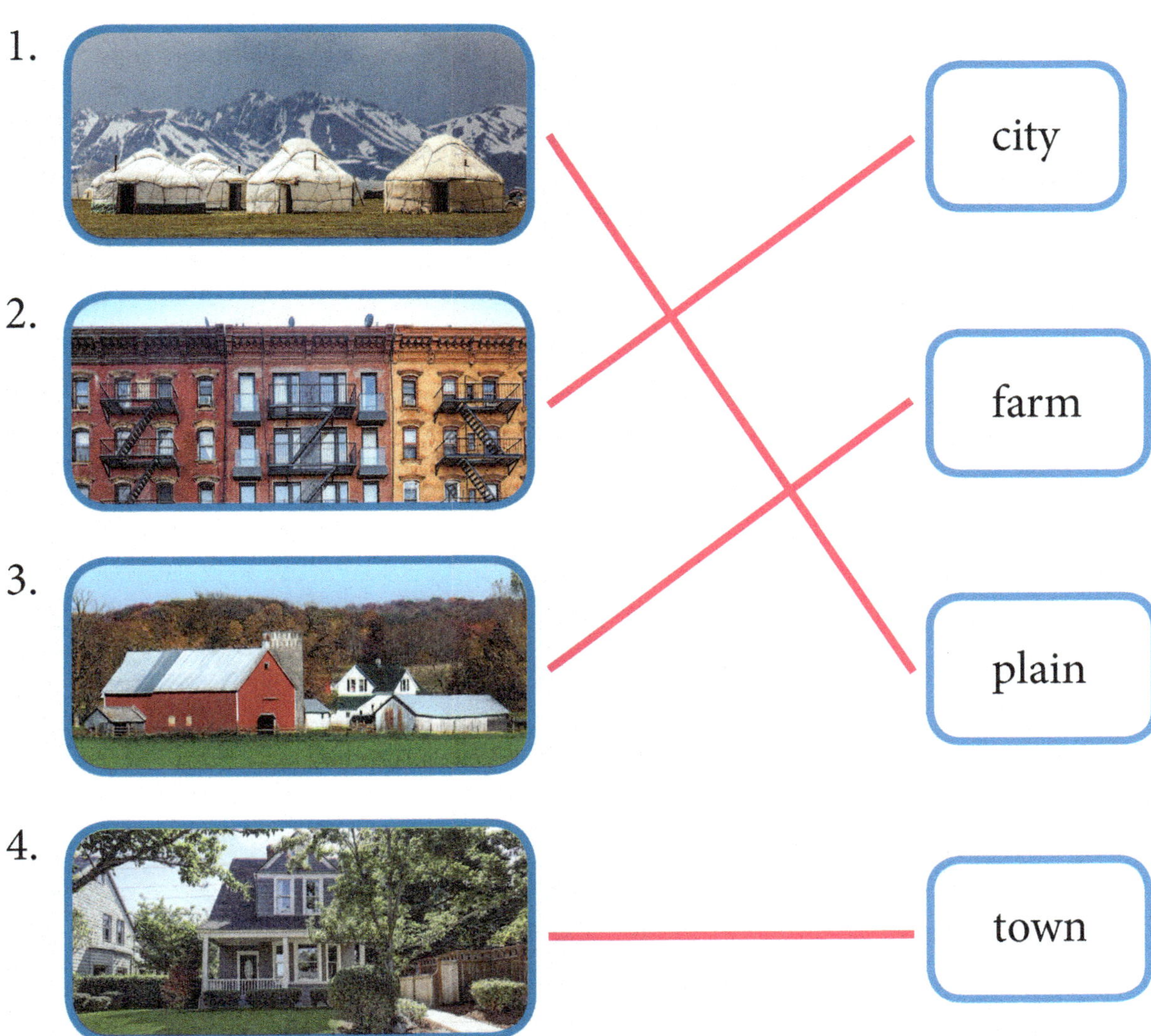

Think of how your life is different from someone else's because of where you live.
Draw a picture of something people like to do in your area.

Family and Community

Addresses

Name ______________________________

Circle Jaylen's house number. Draw a line under the name of his street.

Jaylen Bassey
⑤Main Street
Joliet, IL 60431

Use the map of Main Street to answer the questions.

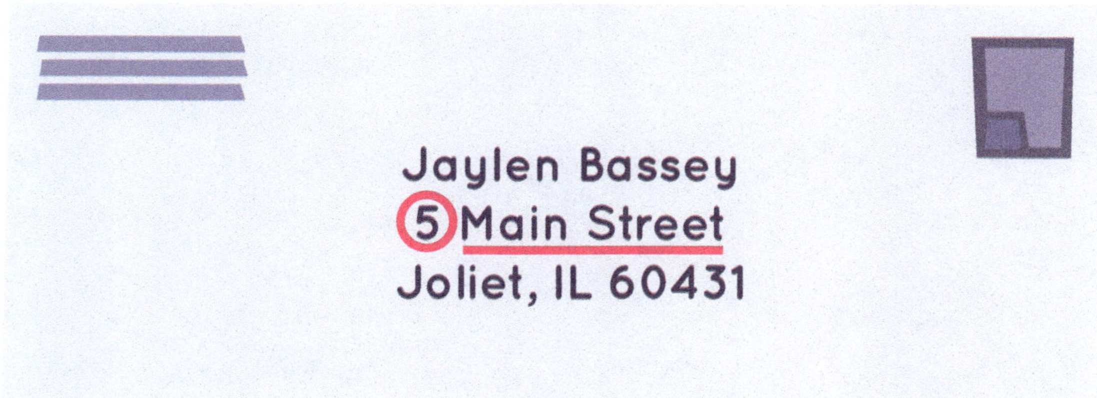

1. What color is Jaylen's house? *yellow*

2. What is the address of the house across the street from Jaylen?

   6 Main Street

3. What color is the house with a mailbox? *red*

4. What is the address of the house with two trees by it?

   4 Main Street

Landmarks

Name ___________________________

Draw a picture of your house. Write the number of your house and the name of the street.

House number __________ Street name ___________________________

Draw a landmark that could help someone find your home.

Christmas Customs

Name ______________________

Look at the pictures of Christmas celebrations in the United States and Germany. Draw a red circle around things that are the same. Draw a blue circle around things that are different.

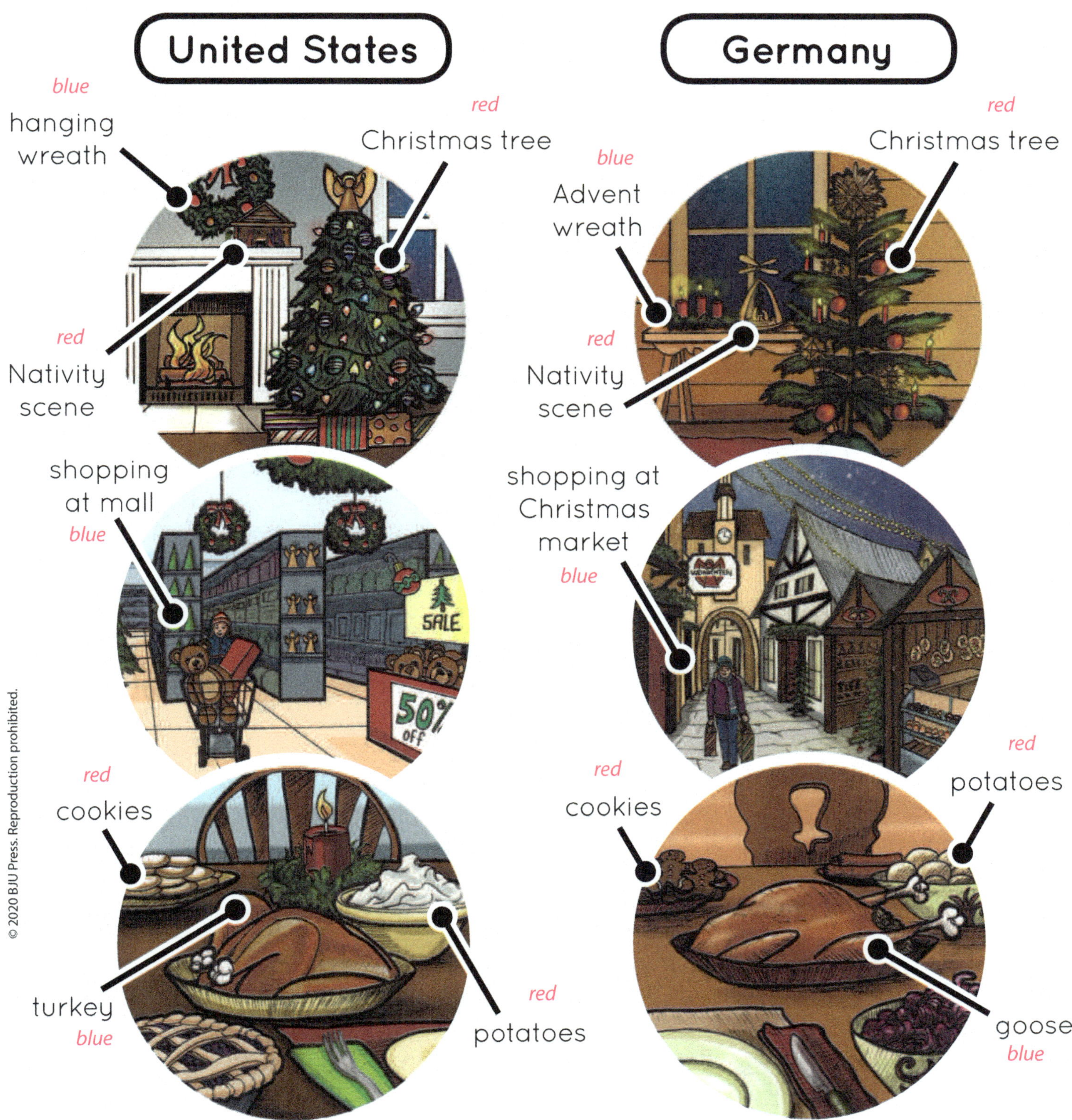

Family Rules

Follow the steps.

1. Read the rules that the parents made for this family.

2. Circle the children who are obeying the rules.

3. Write the number of the reason for the rule in the blank.

   1 The rule helps the family be safe.

   2 The rule helps the family take good care of things.

   3 The rule helps the family be kind.

Family and Community

Compare

Read the paragraphs. Mark all the correct answers.

Families today are like families from the past in some ways. They live together. They work and play together. Parents take care of their children.

Families today are different from families from the past in some ways. They have more tools to help do their work. They can go places faster. They have fun in different ways.

1. How are families today like families from the past?
   - ● They live together.
   - ○ They use the same tools.
   - ● They play together.

2. How are families today different from families from the past?
   - ● They can go places faster.
   - ● They have fun in different ways.
   - ○ Parents take care of their children.

Name ____________________

Write the number of each phrase in the correct part of the Venn diagram.

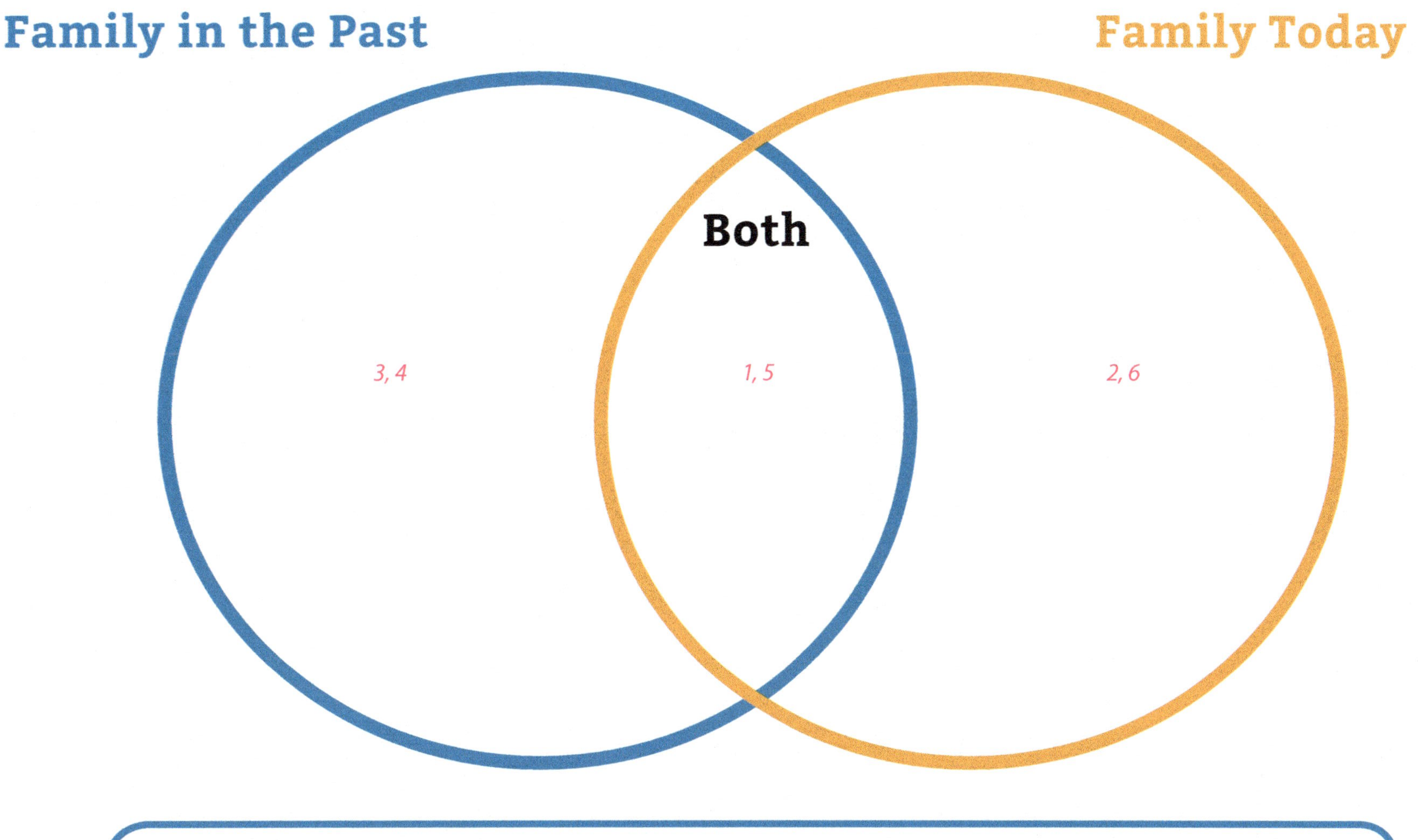

Family and Community

Study Guide

Mark the answer.

1. What word describes Adam and Eve's sin and all the bad things it led to?

   ○ Creation   ● Fall   ○ Redemption

2. What word describes Jesus' payment for sin?

   ○ Creation   ○ Fall   ● Redemption

3. What word describes the time when God made everything?

   ● Creation   ○ Fall   ○ Redemption

Draw a line from the role to the picture of the family member who has the role.

4. Who leads the wife and children to follow God?

5. Who obey their parents?

6. Who helps the husband and also leads the children?

7. People in big cities often live in ____.

   ● apartments   ○ houses

8. People outside big cities often live in ____.

   ○ apartments   ● houses

9. People who herd animals on a plain could live in ____.

   ○ apartments   ● gers

10. A home tells about the ____ of a family.

    ● culture   ○ landmarks

Write the word that completes the sentence.

> **God   love   parents**

11. Families celebrate together to show *love* for each other.

12. The *parents* make rules for the family.

13. Rules help families live how *God* wants them to.

Study Guide

Name _______________________

Draw a line from the vocabulary word to the definition.

14. rules

15. custom

16. home

17. family

a husband and a wife with any children God gives them

what to do and what not to do

the way a group of people does something

where a family lives

Quilt Square

Follow the steps.

1. Use a ruler to draw lines between the matching letters to make the design.

2. Color the sections different colors.

3. Cut out the quilt square to display.

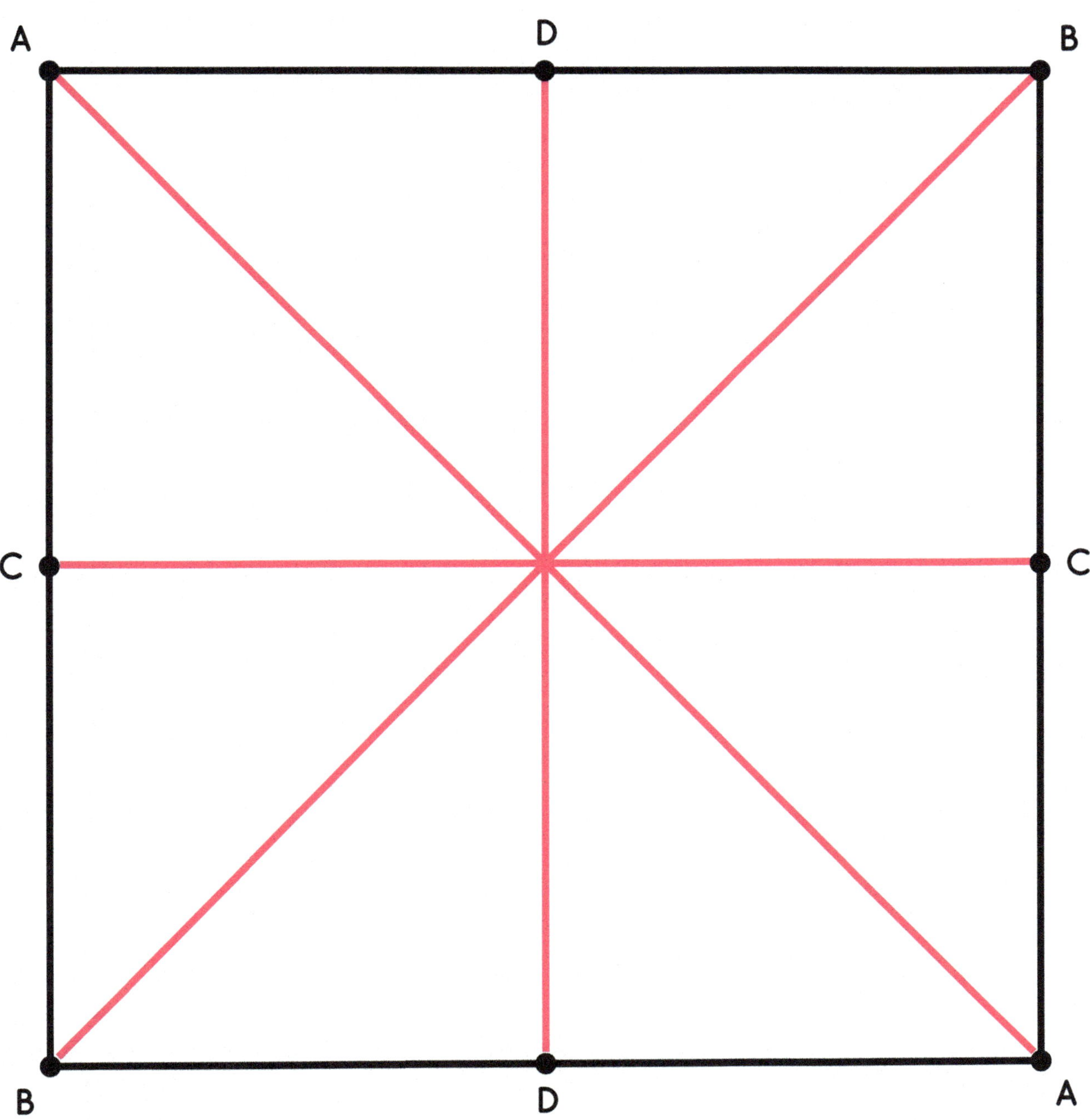

Main Idea and Details

Name ___________________________

1. Read the paragraph.
2. Draw a green line under the sentence that tells the main idea.
3. Draw an orange line under each sentence that gives a detail about the main idea.

A quilting bee was a time to visit and have fun! *1st sentence: underline green*

Women shared news as they made a quilt.

Children snacked on popcorn and apples. They *2nd, 3rd, 4th, 5th sentences: underline orange*

played games. Everyone ate dinner together.

Family and Community

Church Roles

Write the word that completes the sentence. Use the answers to complete the graphic organizer.

> **Christ   members   pastors**

1. The head of the church is _Christ_.

2. The people who lead churches and teach what the Bible says are _pastors_.

3. The people who learn from pastors and serve in the church are _members_.

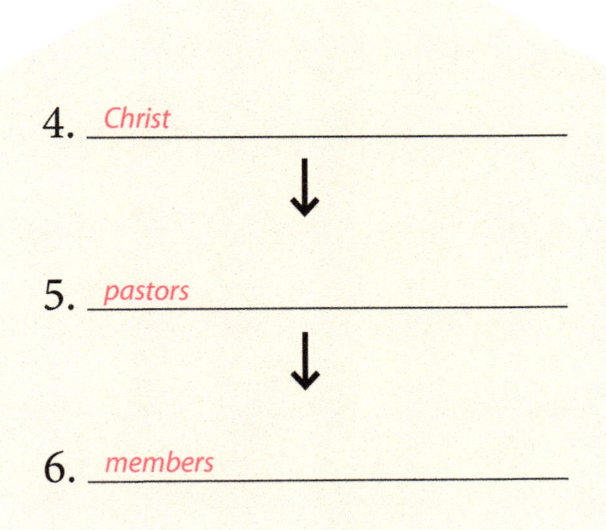

Why Families Should Go to Church

Name ______________________________

Mark the three best reasons why families should go to church.

- ● They will learn about God.
- ○ They will enjoy the playground.
- ● They will learn to love and serve God.
- ● They will learn to love and serve other people.
- ○ They will eat yummy food.

Use the sentences you marked to answer the question.

Why should your family go to church? *Answers should include that my family*

will learn about God, we will learn to love and serve God, and we will learn to love and serve other people.

____

____

School Roles

Write the word that completes the sentence. Use the answers to complete the graphic organizer.

> **God   students   teachers   parents**

1. _God_ planned for children to be taught.

2. God gives _parents_ the job of teaching their children.

3. Children are taught for parents by _teachers_.

4. Parents and teachers teach _students_.

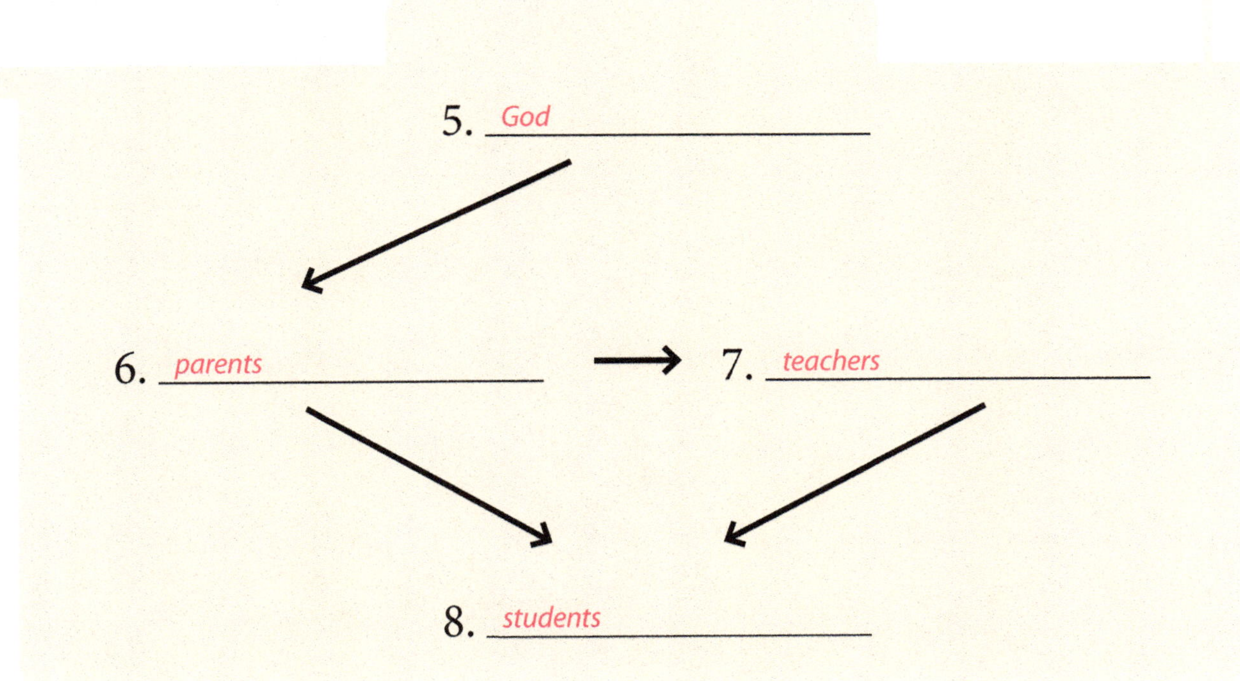

Family and Community

Working Together

Name _________________________

Follow along as your teacher reads the paragraphs. Circle three places the class could visit.

Pretend that your class is planning a field trip. You and your classmates cannot agree on which field trip to take.

Some students want to go to the zoo to see wild animals. Others want to visit a bakery that gives warm cookies to visitors. Some want to visit a fire station where they can sit in a fire engine with flashing lights and a loud siren.

Answer the questions.

1. What can your class hold to decide which field trip to take?

   an election

2. What will each student do to choose a field trip? *vote*

3. What must a field trip have to win? *the most votes*

Follow the steps to make a chart.

1. Write each place you circled in the boxes under *Place.*

2. Write the votes for each field trip under *Votes.*

3. Circle the field trip your class will take.

Class Field Trip

Place	Votes
zoo	
bakery	
fire station	

Government

Mark the answer.

1. What is a law like?

   ○ a choice   ● a rule

2. Who makes laws?

   ● government   ○ parents

3. God wants government to make sure there is what?

   ● justice   ○ conflict

4. What word means that a person is part of a country?

   ○ student   ● citizen

Circle whether the sentence tells a duty or a right.

5. Citizens must obey laws. (duty) right

6. Citizens should be kept safe
   from being hurt by others. duty (right)

7. Citizens must respect the government. (duty) right

8. Citizens should be able to serve God. duty (right)

Government Roles

Name ______________________

Write the word that completes the sentence. Use the answers to complete the graphic organizer.

> **citizens   God   government**

1. _God_________________ planned a way to make sure justice is shown to people.

2. God wants people to have _government_______________ to make sure there is justice.

3. Because of God's plan for government, _citizens_______________ have rights and duties.

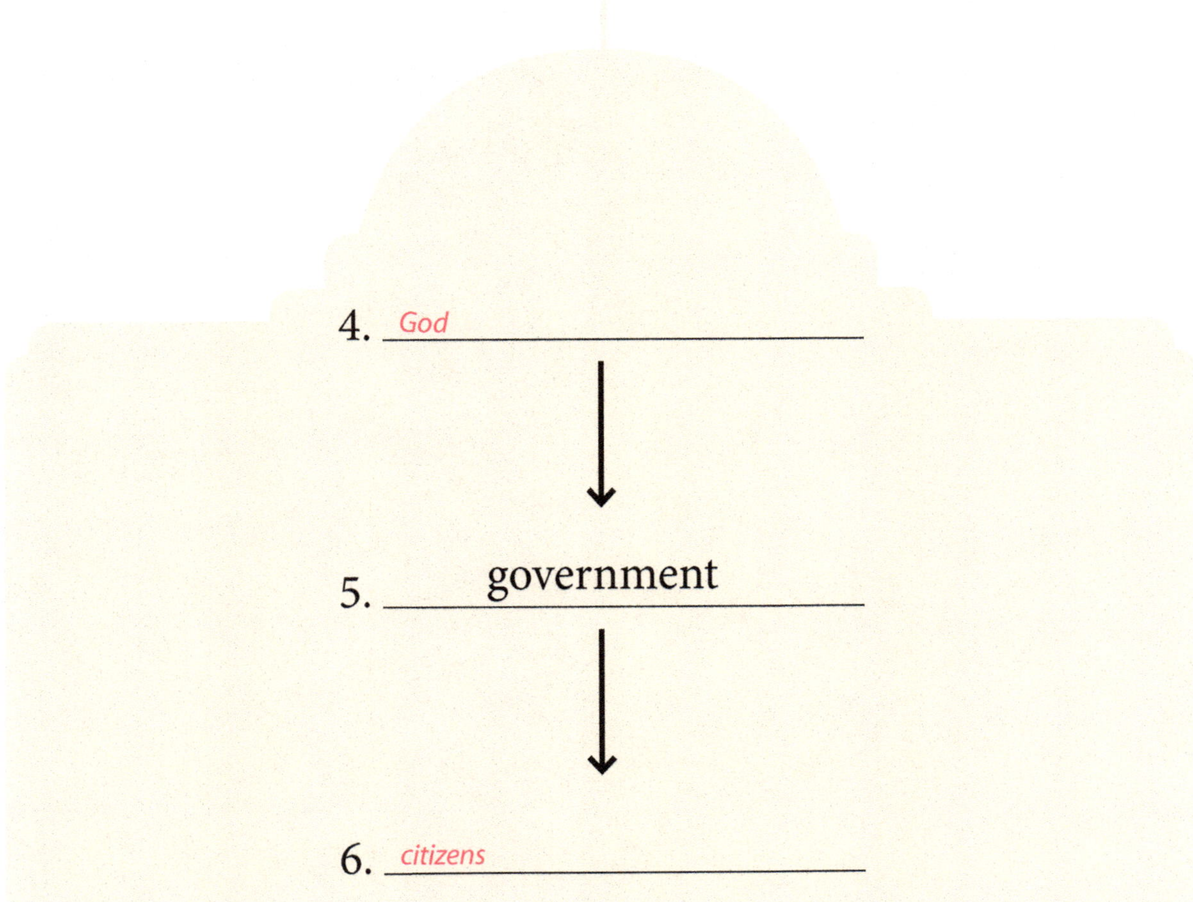

Community Helpers

Name _______________________

1.

2.

3.

4.

5.

Family and Community

Model Community

Name ___________________

Draw a line from the place to the importance of the place.

1. A home — is where people buy the things they need.

2. A church — is where people live.

3. A store — is where people worship God.

4. A park — is where people play.

Glue the pictures from the next page to make a model community. Think about the importance of each place as you arrange the pictures. Write a name for the community.

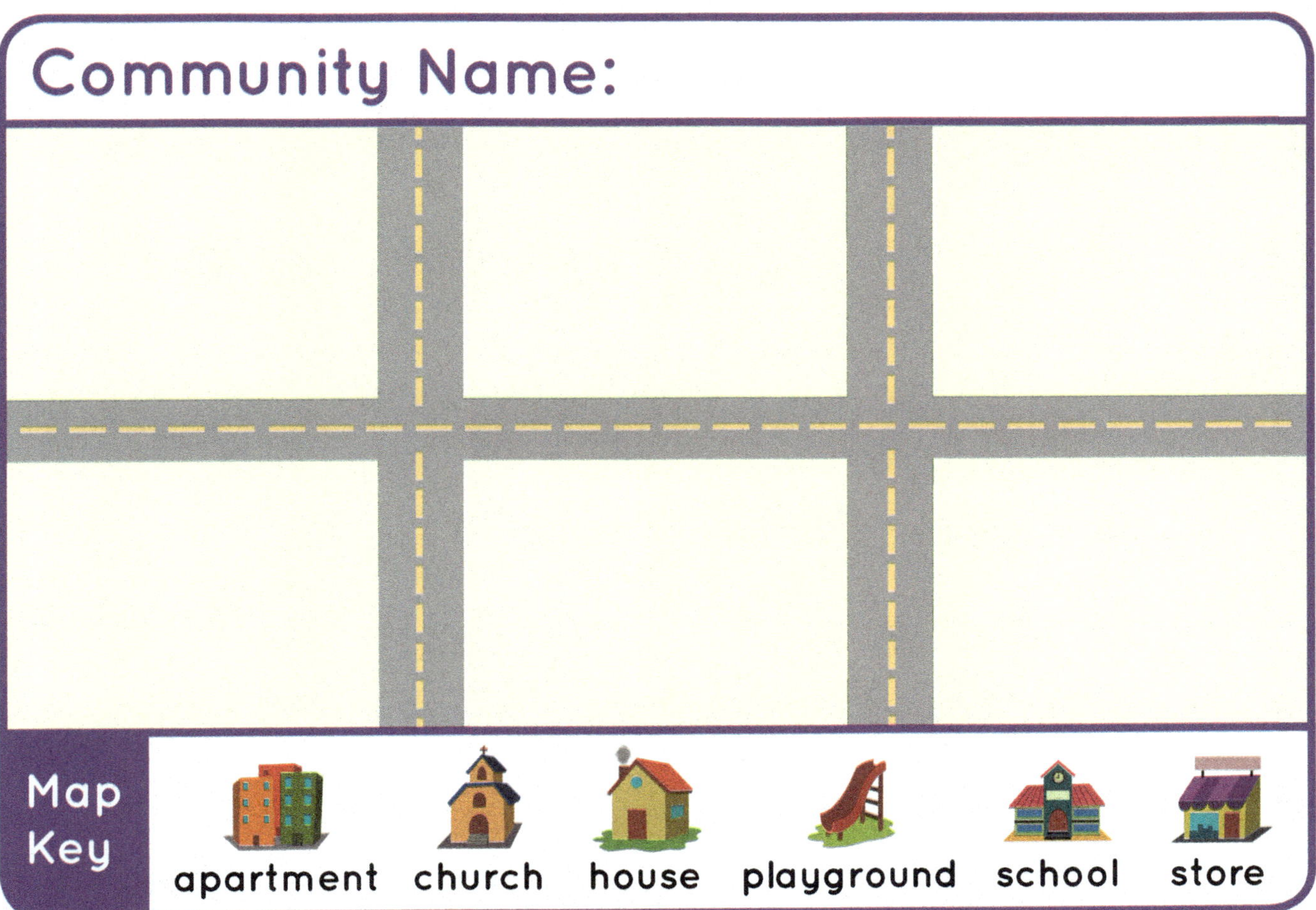

Family and Community

Model Community

Cut out the pictures to make a model community.

Study Guide

Name ___________________________

Write the word that completes the sentence.

> **God   group   needs**

1. A community is a _group_______________ of people who live near each other.

2. _God_________________ wants people to live in communities.

3. People work together to meet each other's _needs_________________.

Draw a line from the description to the correct picture.

4. the people who have trusted in Jesus

5. the people God has told to teach their children

6. a job that students do at school

7. Who leads the church?

8. What is a way a church helps a community?

9. Which picture shows why families should go to church?

Mark the answer.

10. When people disagree, it causes ______.

   ● conflict   ○ happiness

11. One way to make a group decision is to ______.

   ○ argue   ● vote

Name _______________________________

Mark the answer.

12. God wants government to make sure _____ is shown.

    ○ community   ● justice

13. A law is like a _____.

    ● rule   ○ conflict

14. A law is made by _____.

    ○ parents and teachers   ● government

Circle the answer.

15. Which picture shows a citizen?

16. Which picture shows a right?

17. Which picture shows someone obeying the law?

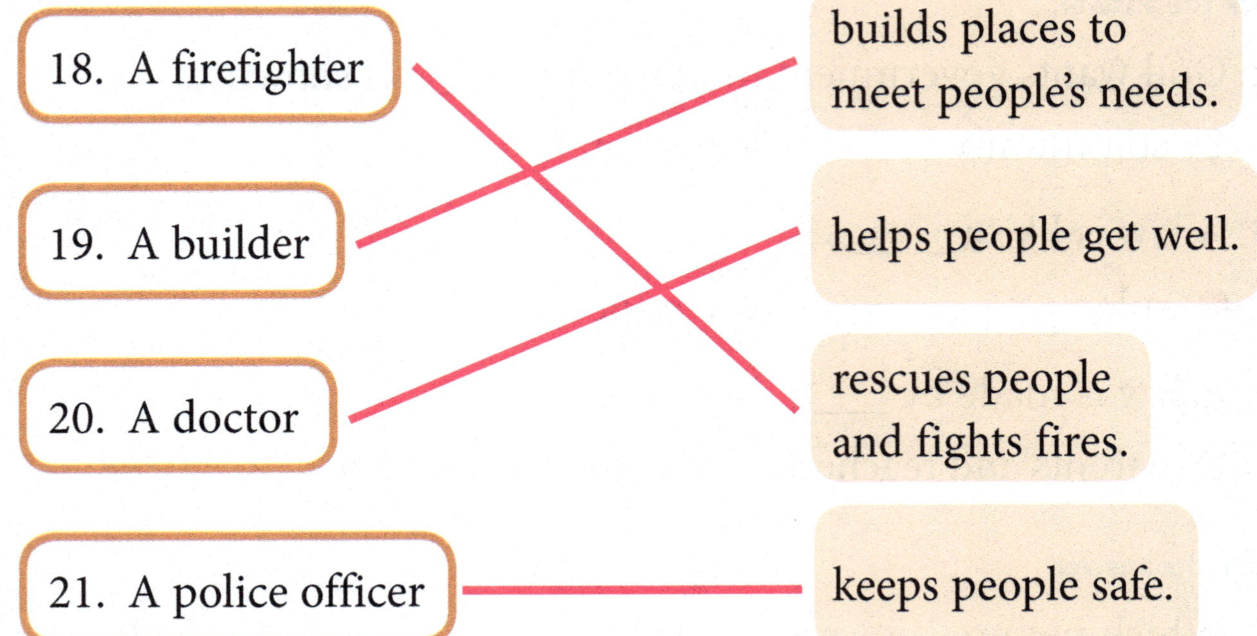

Family and Community

Sorting

Name _______________________

Sort the things into groups by writing the words under what they are used for.

truck

shirt

apple

cheese

rabbit

shoes

dress

crackers

blocks

Clothes	Food	Toys
shirt	*apple*	*truck*
shoes	*cheese*	*rabbit*
dress	*crackers*	*blocks*

Family and Community

Meeting Needs and Wants

Name _______________________

Needs and Wants:

food
knowing God
learning
love
safety
toys

Who Meets Needs and Wants:

church
family
government
school

Write the need or want that each picture shows and write who is meeting the need or want.

1. 

learning

school

2.

toys

family

3. 

food

family

4.

love

family

5.

knowing God

church

6. 

safety

government

Name ___________________________

Glue each picture from the next page in the correct box.

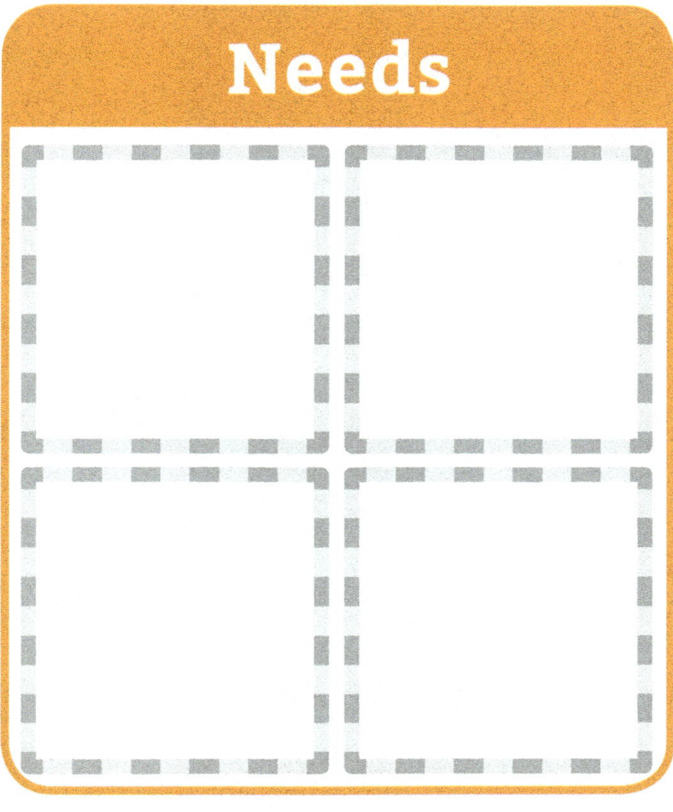

Family and Community

Needs and Wants

Cut out the pictures of needs and wants.

Goods

Name ___________________________

Write the word that completes the sentence.

1. _Needs_ ______________ are things people must have.

2. _Wants_ ______________ are things people would like to have.

3. _Goods_ ______________ are things you can touch that are grown or made.

Mark an X on each good that does not meet a need.

4. 

5. 

6. 

7. 

8. 

9. 

Services

Mark whether people need or want the service in the picture.

1. 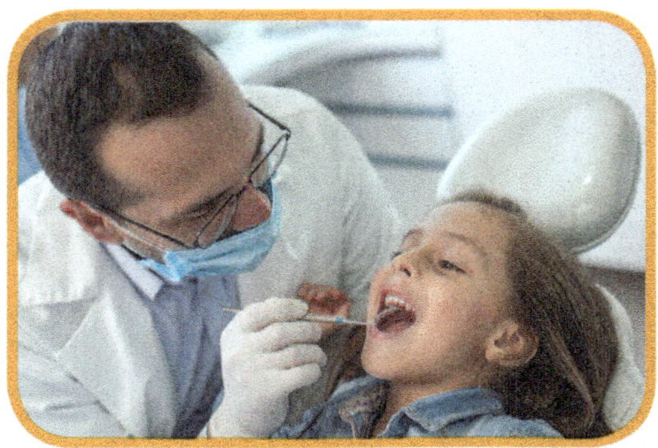

● **need**　　○ want

2. 

○ need　　● **want**

3. 

○ need　　● **want**

4. 

● **need**　　○ want

Draw a picture of someone doing a service. Mark whether the service is a need or a want.

○ need　　　○ want

Producers and Consumers

Name _______________________

Draw a red circle around each producer. Draw a blue circle around each consumer.

1.
red

2.
blue

3.
red

4.
blue

5.
blue

6.
red

Bar Graphs

Use the bar graph to answer the questions.

1. How many dollars does a ball cost? _*three*_______________

2. Which thing costs two dollars? _*jump rope*_____________

3. How many dollars does a teddy bear cost? _*four*__________

4. Which thing costs the most dollars? _*crayons*__________

5. Which thing costs less than a ball? _*jump rope*__________

Planning What You Buy

Name _______________________

Follow the steps. Be sure that you do not use more than ten dollars.

1. Color one block for each dollar you will give to your church.

2. Color one block for each dollar you will save.

3. Choose birthday gifts for two friends. Color one block for each dollar you will spend to buy the gifts.

Dollars	Give to church	Save	Coloring book $3	Ball $3	Stuffed animal $2
5					
4					
3					
2					
1					

Name ___________________________

Draw a line from the sentence to the picture that completes it.

1. If you like animals, you might want to be a ____.

2. If you like school, you might want to be a ____.

3. If you like to cook, you might want to be a ____.

4. If you like sports, you might want to be a ____.

5. If you like the outdoors, you might want to be a ____.

Draw a picture of a job you would like to have.

Serving in a Job

Name ______________________

Pick up sticks in the yard: $2

Pull weeds in the flower bed: $3

Help wash the car: $2

Rake the leaves: $3

Sweep the porch: $3

Write the amount of money you will earn for each job. Add the numbers together.

Jobs Chosen	Money Earned
Total	$

Will you make at least eight dollars? ______________

Tools

Draw a line from the worker to the tool he or she would use.

1.  doctor

2.  farmer

3.  music teacher

4.  photographer

5.  pilot

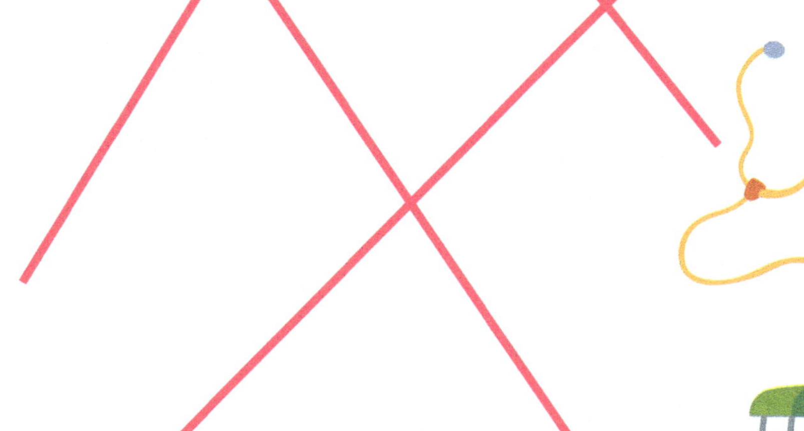

Name _______________

Circle the word that completes the sentence.

1. _____ buy goods and services.   (**Consumers**)   Producers

2. _____ are things you can touch.   Services   (**Goods**)

3. _____ make and sell goods and services.   Consumers   (**Producers**)

4. _____ help people by doing things for them.   (**Services**)   Goods

5. _____ are people who do not get paid for their work.   Inventors   (**Volunteers**)

Write the word that completes the sentence.

> **barter   money   nurse   problems   stove**

6. Trading your apple for a friend's banana is an example of a _barter_ .

7. Most people trade _money_ for goods and services.

8. Jobs help people by solving _problems_ .

9. If you like to take care of sick and hurt people, you might want to be a _nurse_ .

10. If you were a cook, you would use a _stove_ .

11. *blue*

12. *red*

13. *blue*

14. *blue*

15. *red*

16. *red*

Draw a green circle around each service. Draw an orange circle around each good.

17. *green*

18. *orange*

19. *green*

20. *orange*

Family and Community

Caring for God's World   Name _______________________

1.  

2.  

3.  

Family and Community

Landforms and Bodies of Water

Draw a line from the landform to its definition.

1. plain

2. hill

3. mountain

4. desert

land that rises up

a large area of land with steep sides

low, flat land with few trees

very dry land that can be hot or cold

Draw a line from the landform to its picture.

5. plain

6. hill

7. mountain

8. desert

Family and Community

Lesson 41

Draw a line from the body of water to its definition.

9. ocean

10. lake

11. river

a body of water with land all around it

water that flows through land

a large body of salt water

Draw a line from the body of water to its picture.

12. ocean

13. lake

14. river

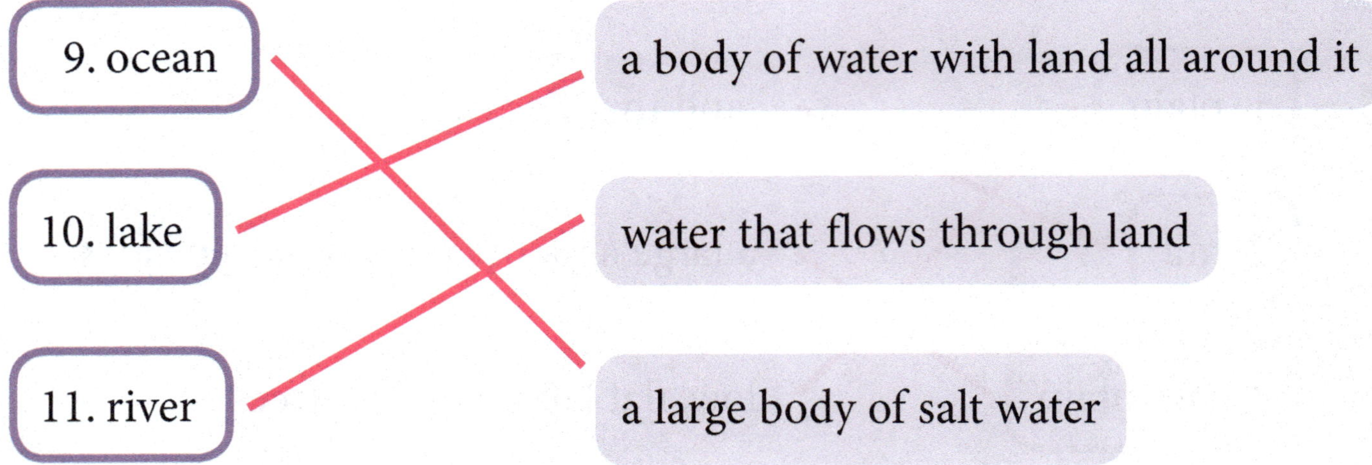

Family and Community

The Globe

Label the globe with the four main directions.

east
north
south
west

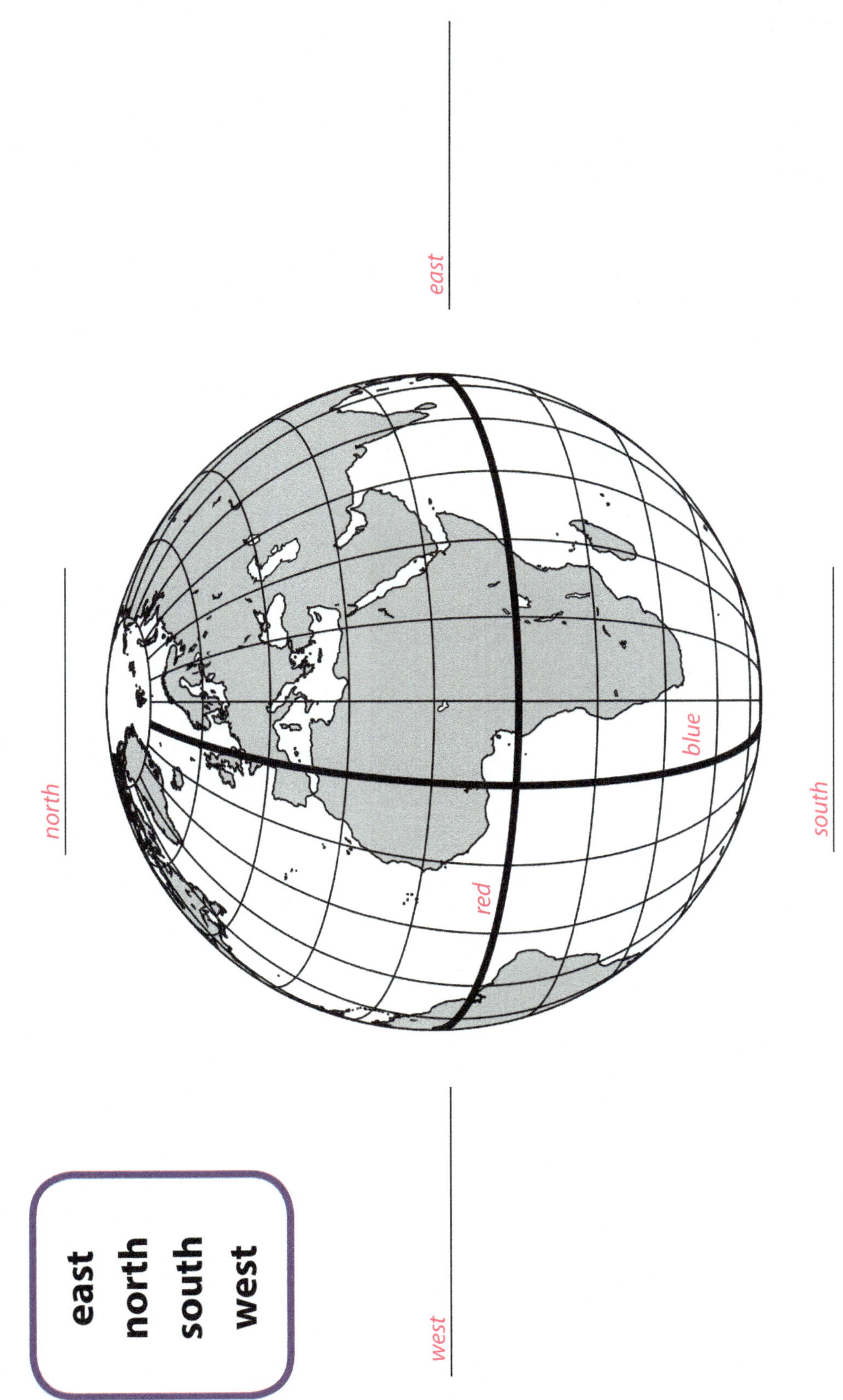

Follow the steps.

1. Use a red crayon to trace the bold line that runs east and west on the globe.

2. Use a blue crayon to trace the bold line that runs north and south on the globe.

1. What shape is a globe?

2. What is a globe a model of?

3. What shows directions on a globe?

the earth

compass rose

round

The Globe: Continents and Oceans

Name ______________________________

Atlantic   North   Pacific   South

1. *North* ______________
   America

*Arctic
Ocean*

2. *Atlantic* ______________
   Ocean

Europe

Africa

3. *Pacific* ______________
   Ocean

4. *South* ______________
   America

Family and Community   Lesson 43   **87**

Family and Community

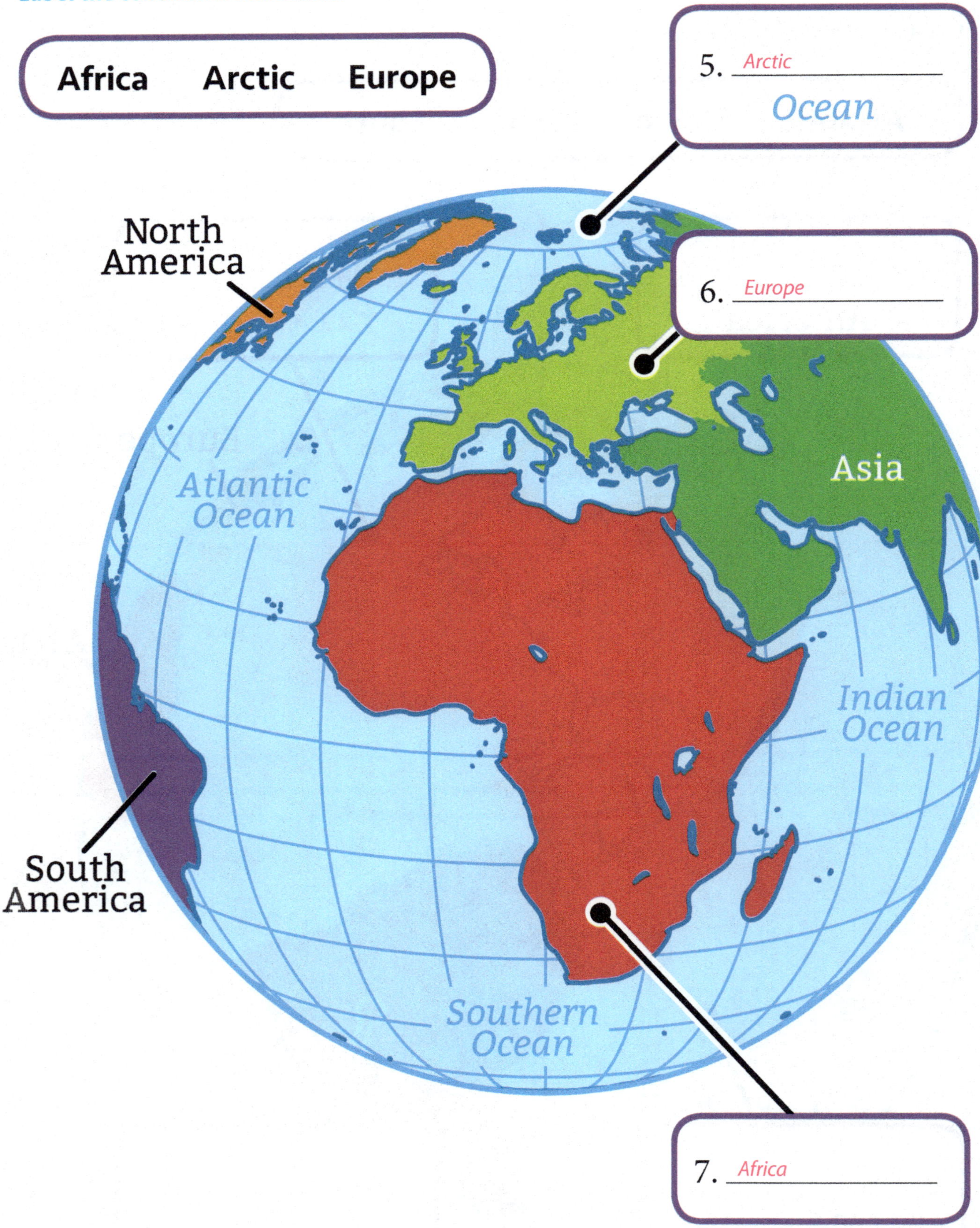

The Globe: Continents and Oceans

Name _______________________

Antarctica   Australia   Southern

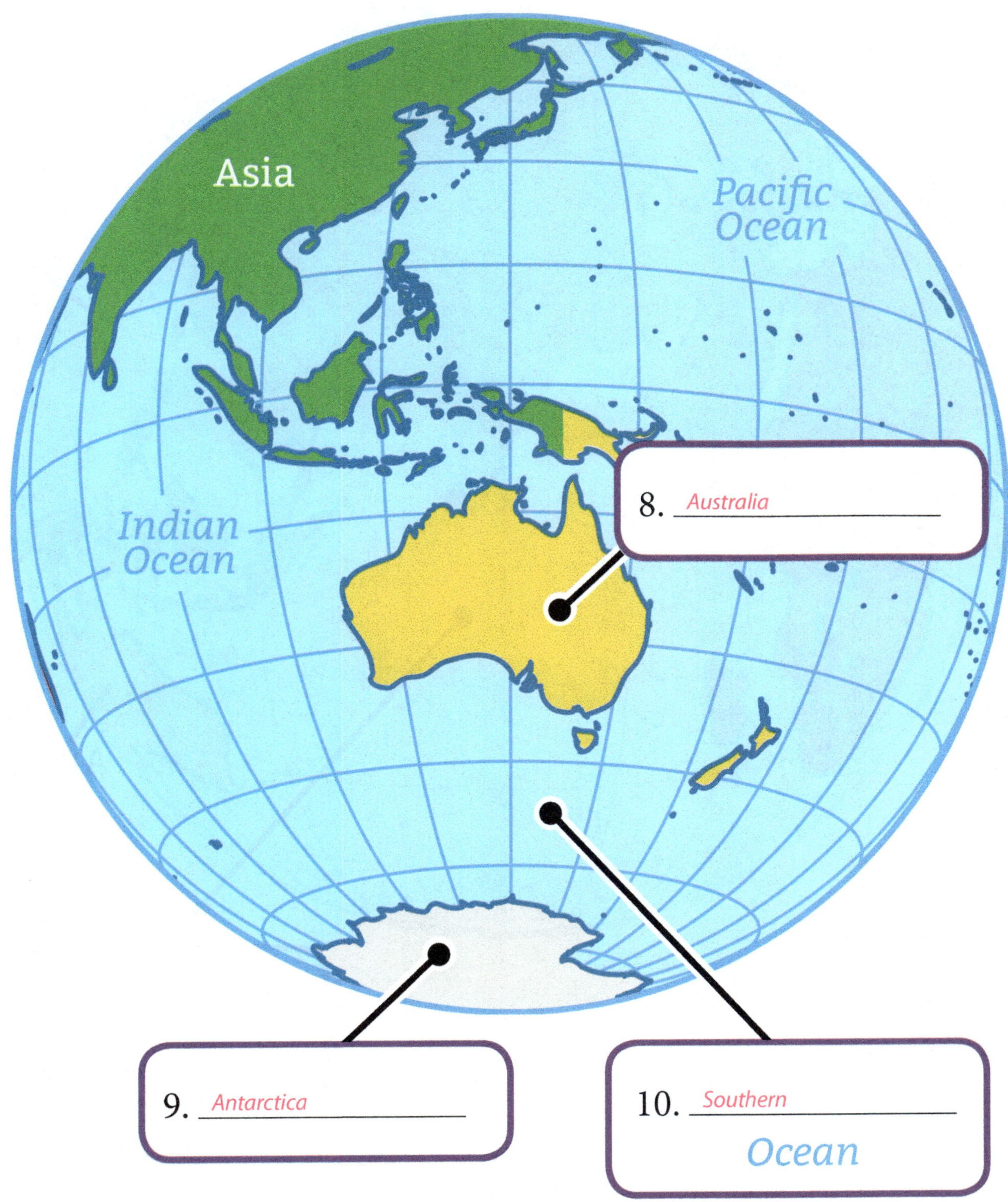

Asia   Indian

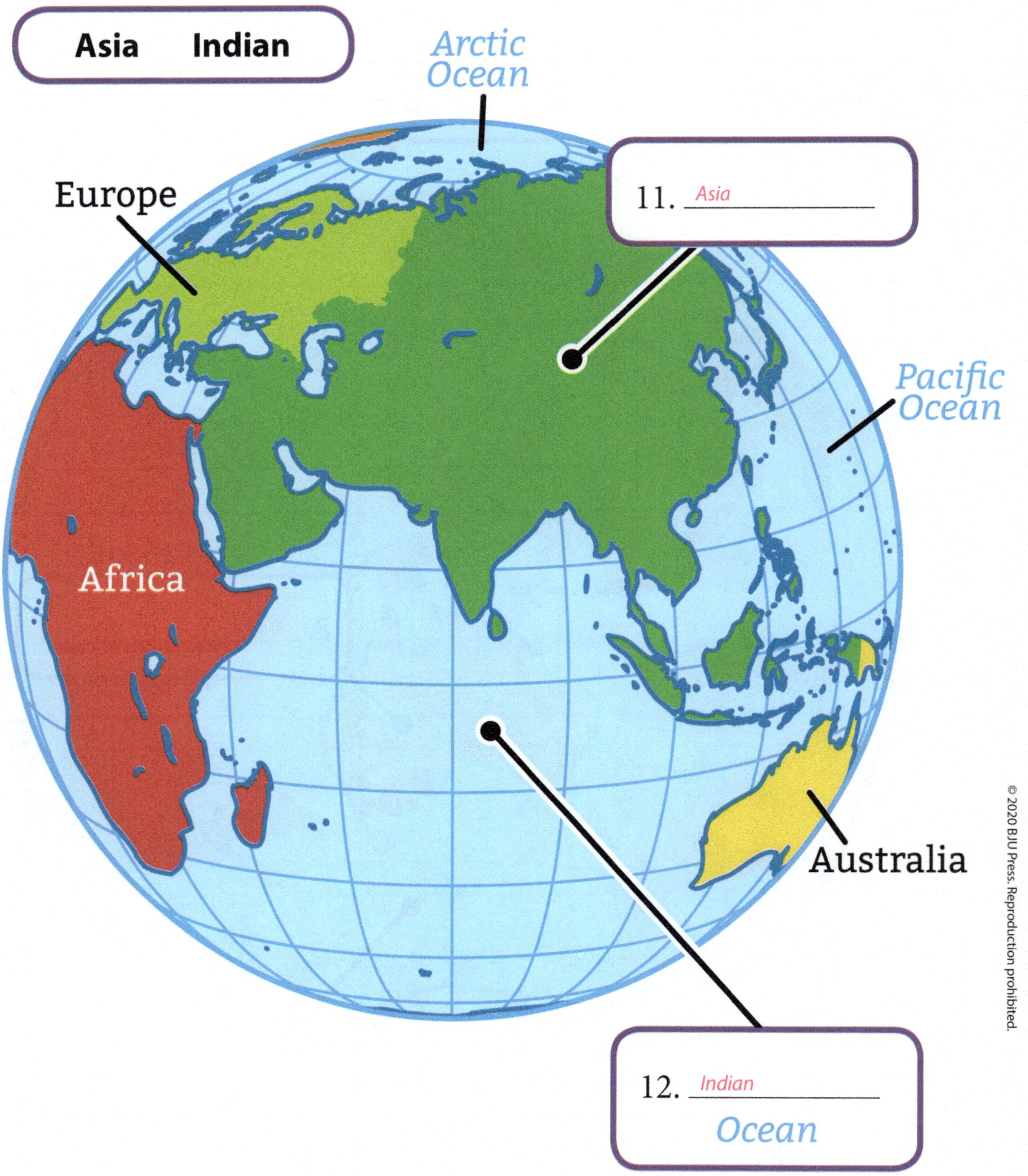

    Family and Community

Map of the Earth: Oceans and Continents

Name ___________________________

Label the oceans.

Arctic   Atlantic   Indian   Pacific   Southern

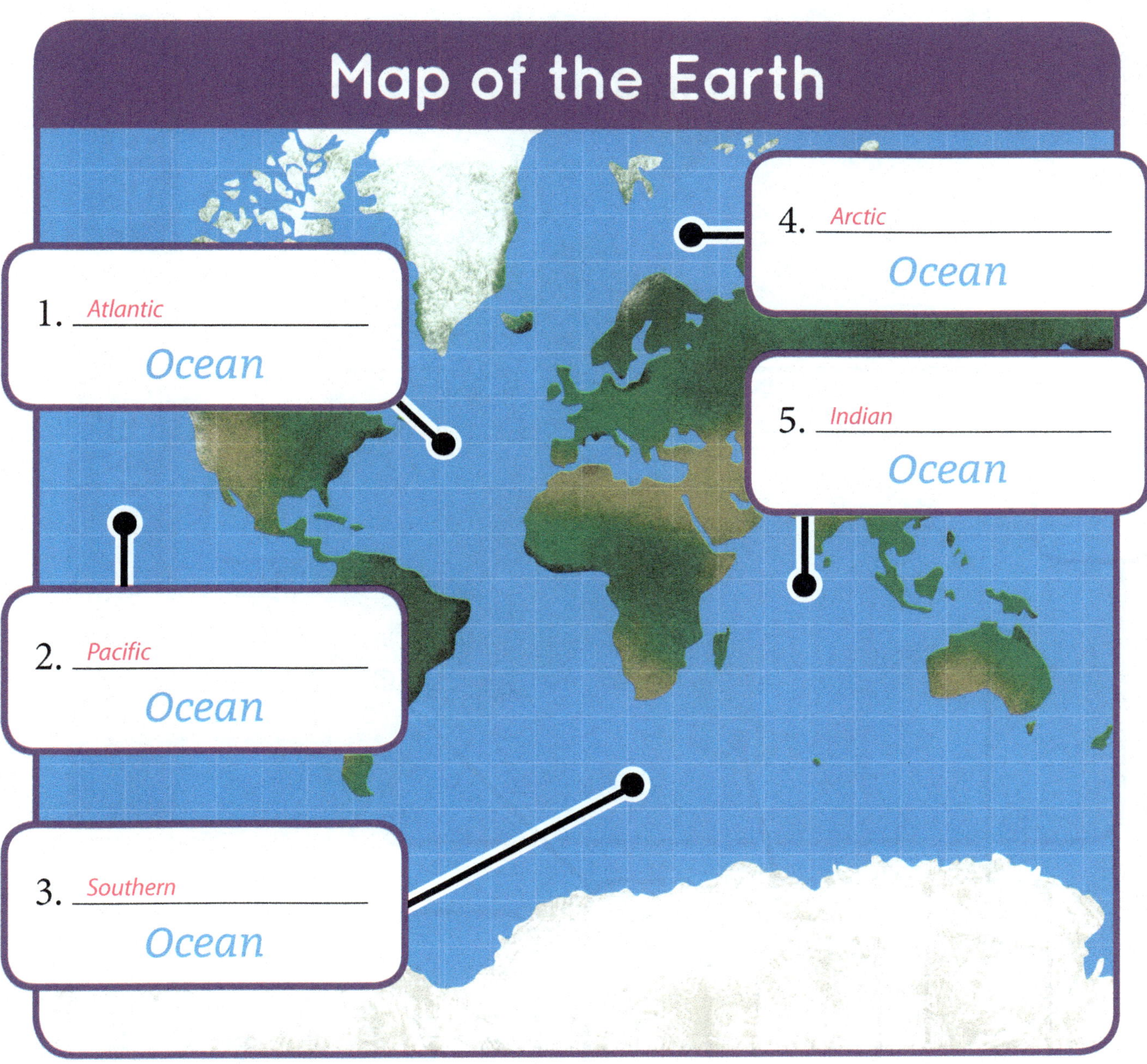

Label the continents.

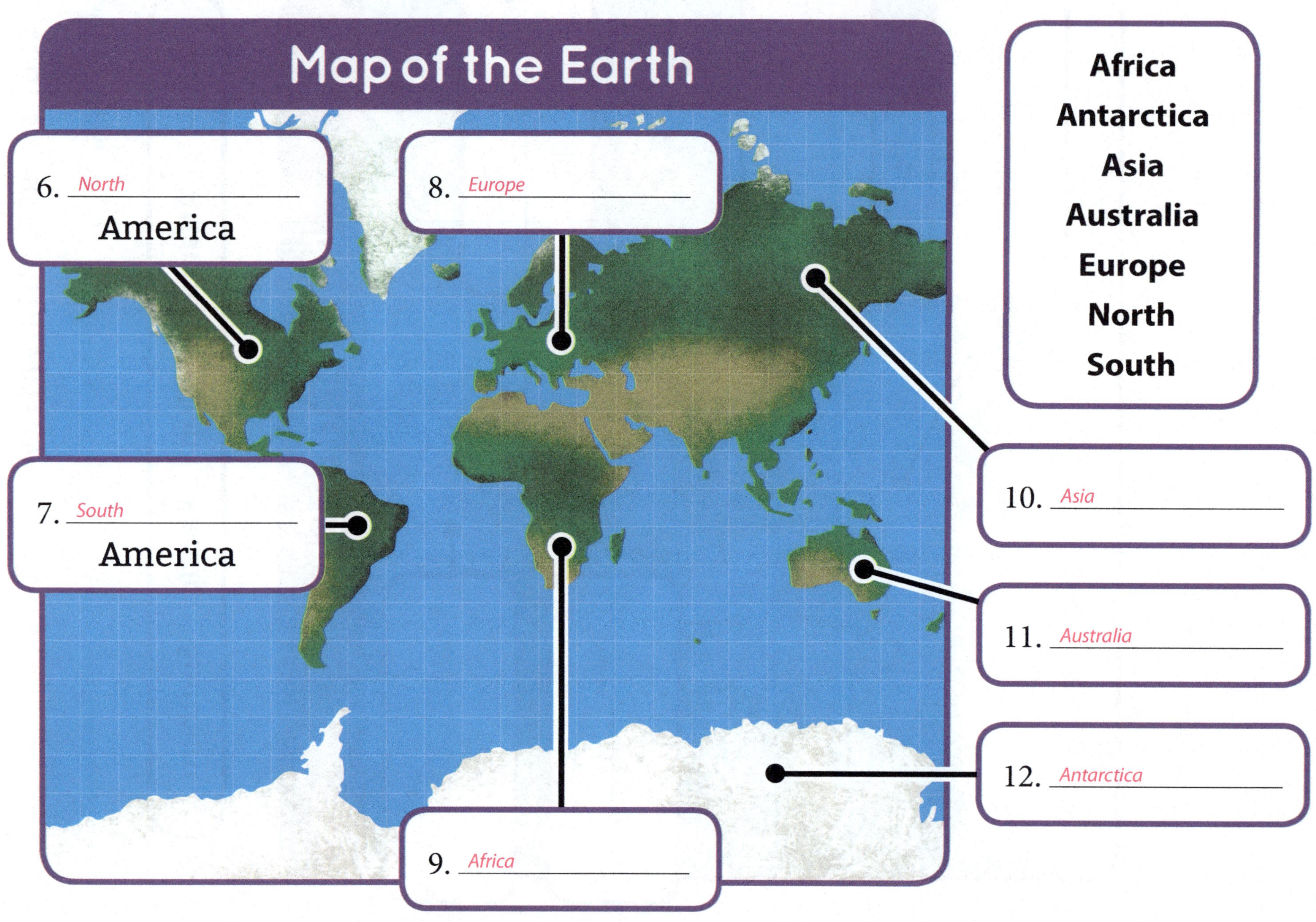

My Map

Name _______________________________

Map title _______________________________

Family and Community

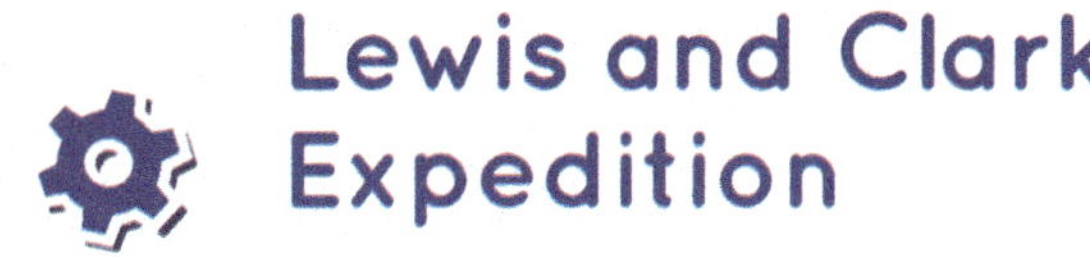

Lewis and Clark Expedition

Name ___________________________

Draw an *X* on the map where Lewis and Clark began their trip.

Use the map to answer the questions.

1. What is the name of the city where they began their trip?

   St. Louis

2. What direction did Lewis and Clark travel? *west*

3. What mountains did they cross? *Rocky Mountains*

4. What ocean is west of the Rocky Mountains?

   Pacific Ocean

5. What mountains would Lewis and Clark have reached if they had gone east from St. Louis?

   Appalachian Mountains

6. What ocean is east of St. Louis? *Atlantic Ocean*

7. What lakes are north of St. Louis? *Great Lakes*

Name _______________________

Number the steps to match the order shown in the diagram.

___4___ The water falls from the clouds to the ground.

___2___ The sun warms the water and moves it up.

___1___ The water goes into the air.

___3___ The water forms clouds.

Water Cycle

Using Resources Wisely

Circle the picture in each row that shows a wise use of resources.

1.  

2.  

3.  

Ways to Save and Use Resources

1. I will reduce the amount of paper I use.

2. I will reuse my old toys.

3. I will recycle my old clothing.

Ways to Save and Use Resources

Cut out a picture from each set.

Name _______________________

Mark the answer.

1. How does the Bible teach us to use God's world?

  ● wisely   ○ harmfully

Circle the answer.

2. Which picture shows how people change the land as they use it?

3. Which picture shows a plain?

4. Which picture shows a mountain?

5. Which picture shows a river?

6. What are the largest bodies of water on the earth?   oceans   lakes

7. What are the biggest areas of land on the earth?   hills   continents

Label the continents and oceans.

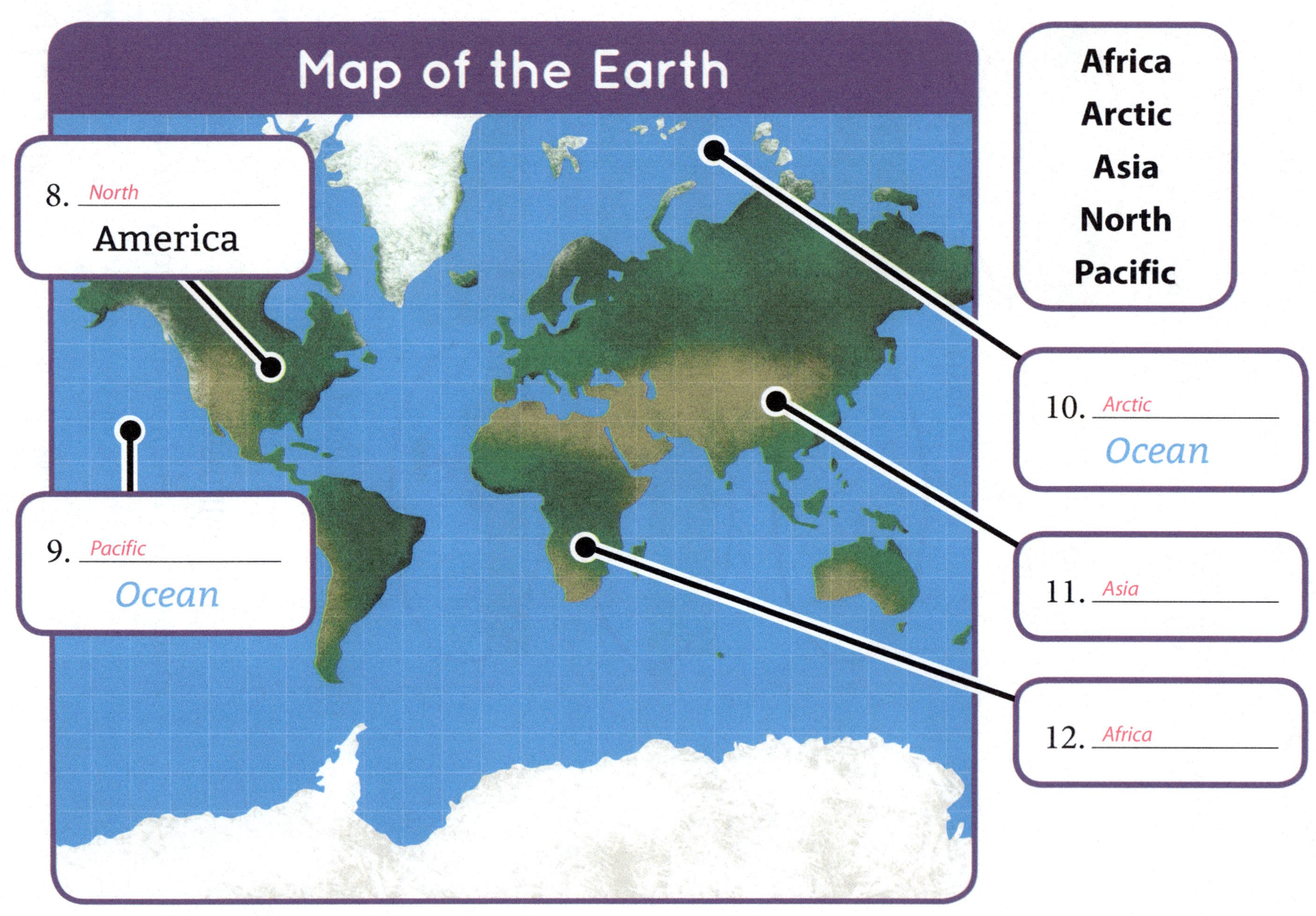

Name _______________________

Circle all the answers.

13. What are the four main directions we use to locate places on the earth?

west   south   up   east   north

Mark the answer.

14. What is a globe a model of?

● the earth   ○ space

15. What do we call the process of water moving from the earth to the sky and back to the earth again?

○ seasons   ● water cycle

16. Which is a natural resource found on the earth?

● land   ○ toys

17. Which is a reason people should use resources wisely?

● Resources belong to God because He made the world.

○ There are a lot of resources.

18. How can people show love to others as the Bible tells us to?

○ Use up all the earth's resources.

● Save resources for others to use in the future.

19. What is a way you save resources at home?

○ I let the water run while I brush my teeth.

● I turn off the water while I brush my teeth.

Fact and Opinion

Name _______________________

Read the paragraph. Draw a line through the sentence that is an opinion.

Chinese Americans worked on a very long railroad. They started in the west. Other workers started in the east. They worked until they met. People could ride all the way across the country. ~~I think it was the best railroad in the world.~~

Mark the answer.

How do you know the sentence you crossed out is an opinion?

○ The sentence is true for everyone.

● The sentence is what one person thinks.

Find and color your state.

Your State

Name ______________________________

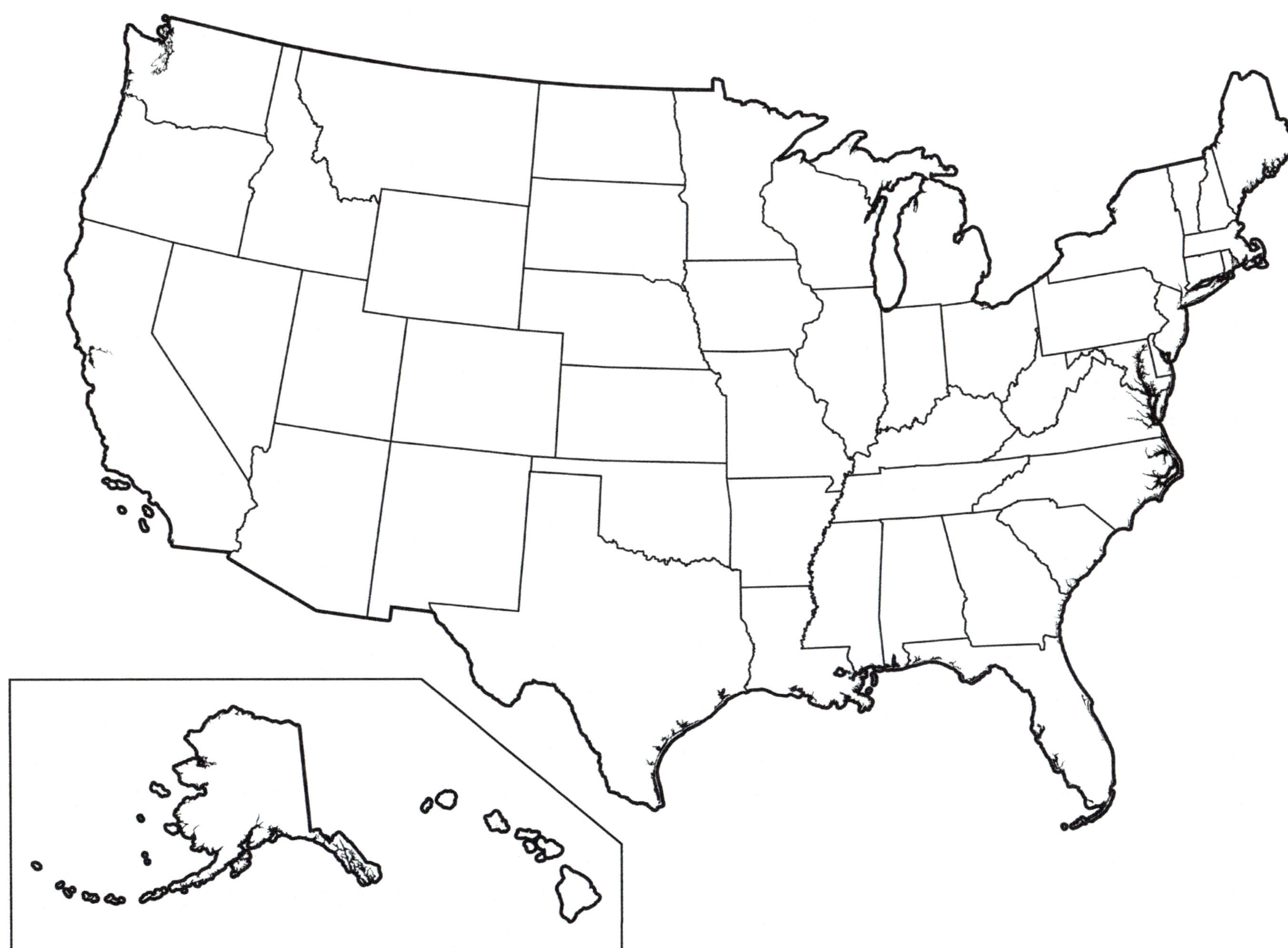

1. What is the capital of your state? _______________________

2. What other states touch your state? _______________________

____

____

3. What large bodies of water are close to your state?

____

____

4. What is one special thing to see or do in your state?

____

5. What is your state bird? _______________________

6. What is your state flower? _______________________

Draw your state flag.

                                    Family and Community

Timelines

Name ______________________

1. Cut apart the timeline. Glue the two parts together.

2. Glue the completed timeline onto a sheet of paper.

3. Cut apart the pictures below or bring your own pictures.

4. Arrange the pictures from youngest to oldest.
   Start on the left.

5. Glue the pictures next to the timeline.
   Draw a line from each picture to the age it shows.

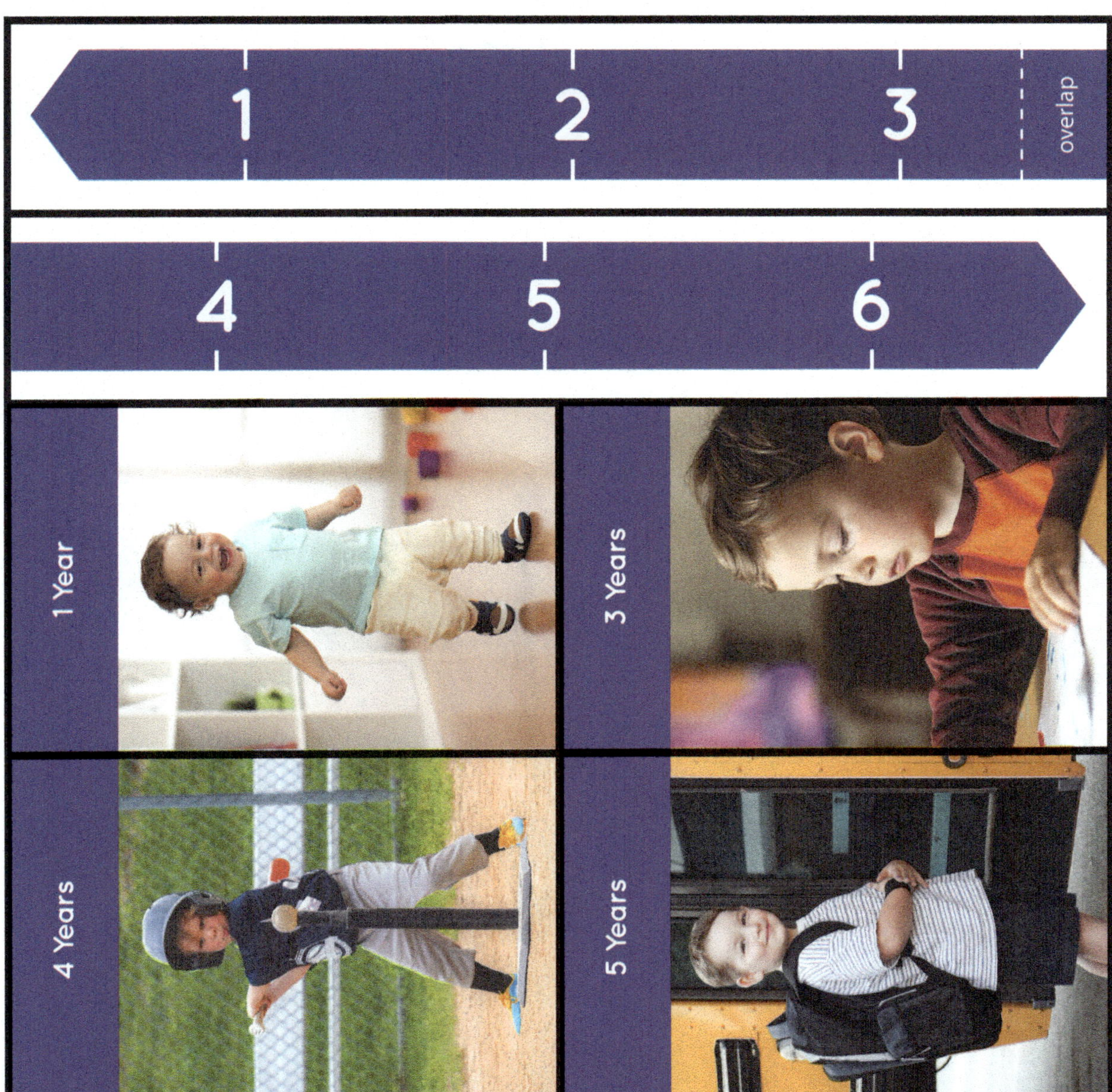

Family and Community

Planning a Vacation

Name ___________________________

Follow the steps to plan a family vacation.

1. Look at the picture map of the United States. Draw four places you would like to visit.

2. Sequence the four places in the order you would like to visit them.

3. Write your first stop on the timeline by number one. Write the next stops in order by two, three, and four.

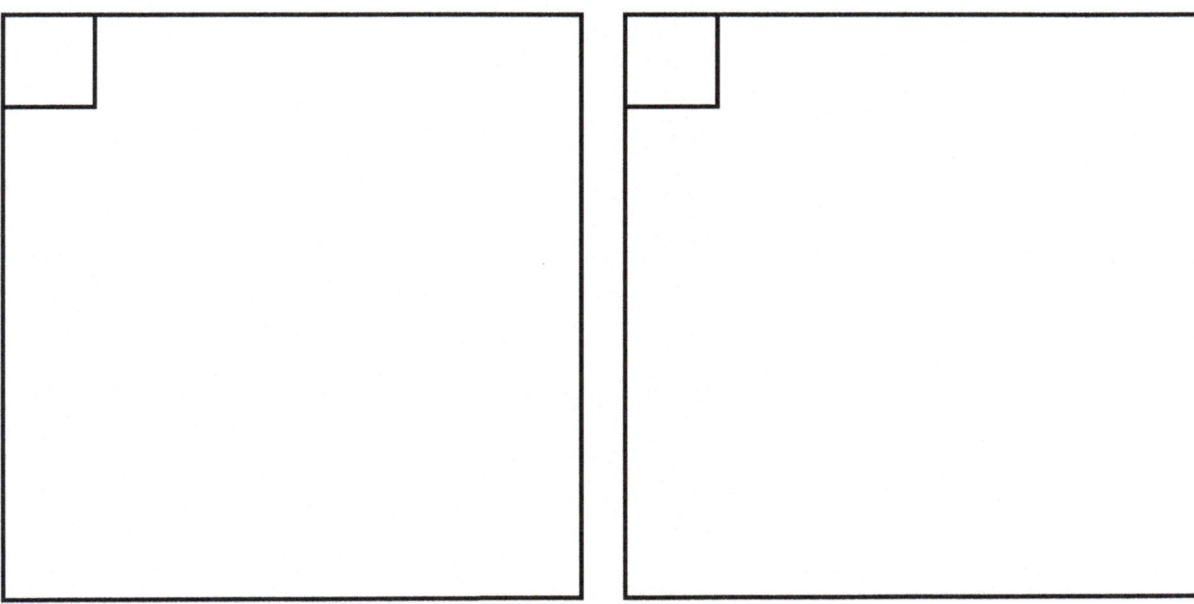

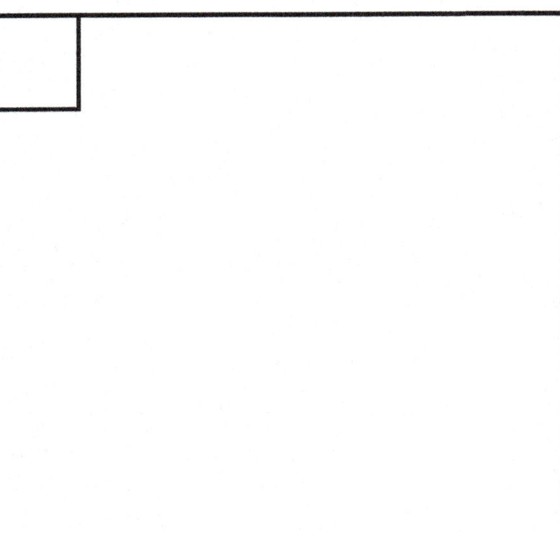

Family and Community

Planning a Vacation

Your Country's Neighbors and Capital

Name _______________________

Follow the steps.

1. Color the United States of America blue.

2. Color Canada red.

3. Color Mexico green.

4. Color the star for Washington, DC, yellow.

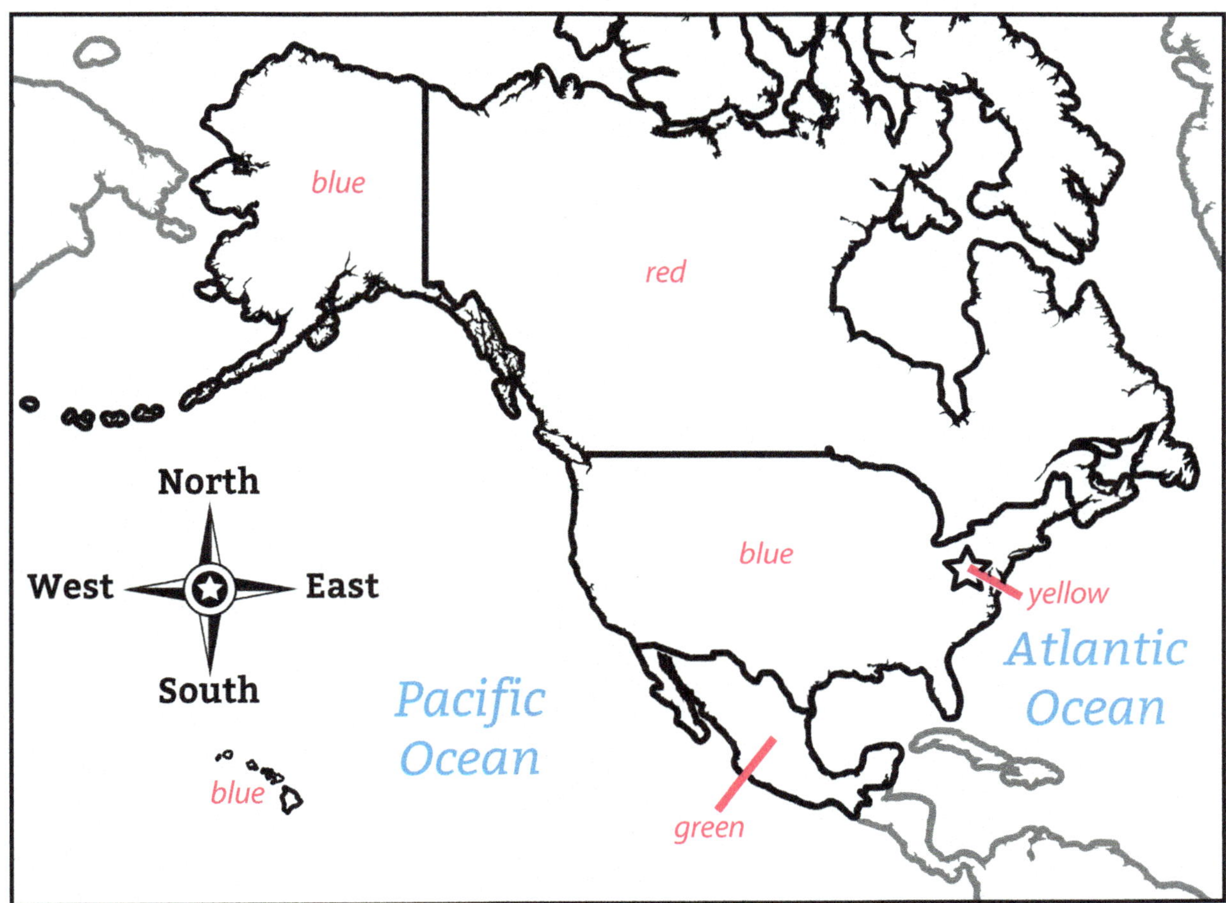

Circle the word that completes the sentence.

1. Mexico is north / **south** of the United States.

2. Canada is **north** / south of the United States.

American Rights and Responsibilities

Name _______________________

1. meet together
2. obey the laws
3. show respect for leaders

4. speak and write things
5. show respect for other citizens
6. worship God

Look at the picture and read the caption. Decide whether they show a right or a responsibility. Write the right or responsibility from numbers 1–6.

Ben stops when the light turns red.

7. _obey the laws_

____

Jaylen wants his neighbor to be safe.

8. _show respect for other citizens_

____

The Johnsons go to church.

9. _worship God_

____

Emma tells about her plan to help her school.

10. _speak and write things_

____

American Symbols and Pledge

Name ______________________

Draw a line from the symbol to its picture.

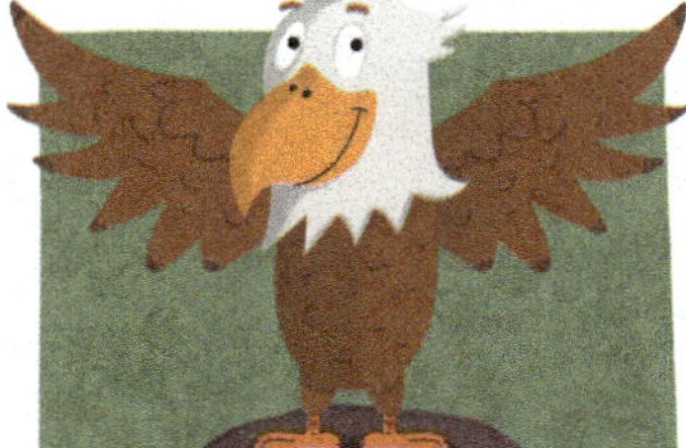

1. American flag

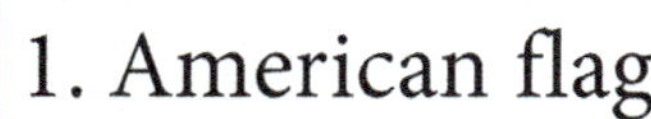

2. bald eagle

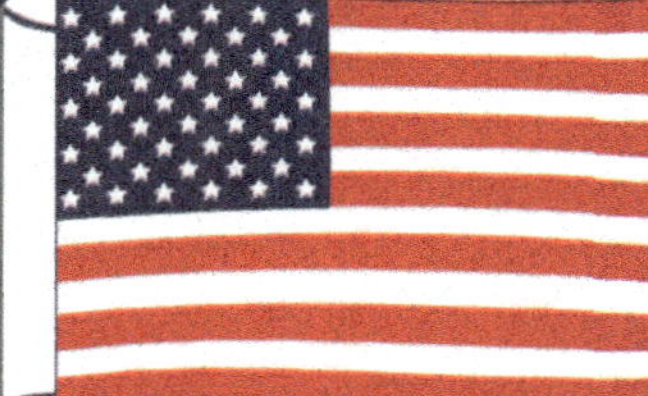

3. Statue of Liberty

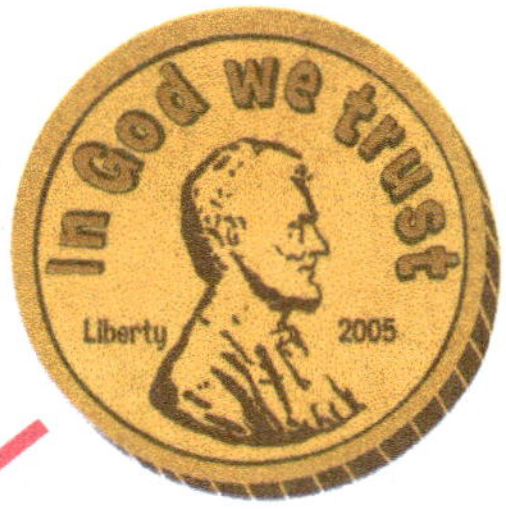

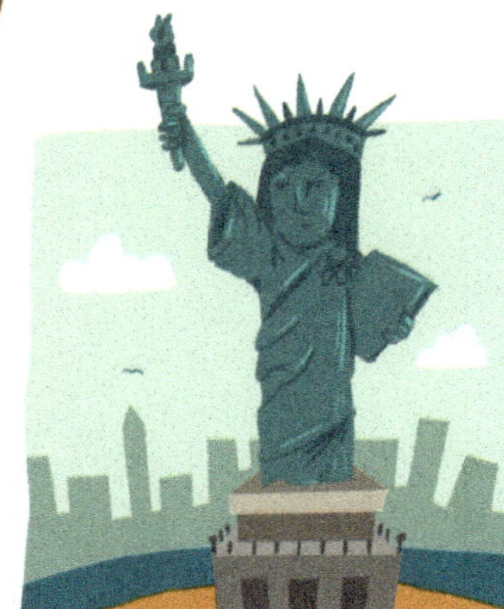

4. United States motto

Write the words to complete the Pledge of Allegiance.

all **Flag** **God** **pledge** **stands**

I *pledge* allegiance to the *Flag* of the United States of America, and to the Republic for which it *stands*, one Nation under *God*, indivisible, with liberty and justice for *all*.

The President

Name ______________________

Write the word or words that best complete each description of the president.

fairly   laws   United States   White House

1. lives in the

   White House

2. makes sure people obey the

   laws

the president

3. is the leader of the

   United States

4. helps the government be sure people are treated

   fairly

Answer the questions.

5. Who is the president? ______________________

6. Think about the things a good leader does. What is one thing you would do if you were the president?

____

____

Study Guide

Name ______________________________

Write the word or words that complete the sentence.

> **Canada   freedom   Mexico
> United States   Washington, DC**

1. Our country's name is the _United States_____________.

2. _Canada___________________ is north of our country.

3. _Mexico___________________ is south of our country.

4. Our country's capital is _Washington, DC_____________.

5. Our country gives people _freedom_______________.

Draw a blue circle around each right. Draw a red circle around each responsibility.

6. meet together *blue*

7. obey the laws *red*

8. show respect for other citizens *red*

9. worship God *blue*

Draw a line from the vocabulary word to the definition.

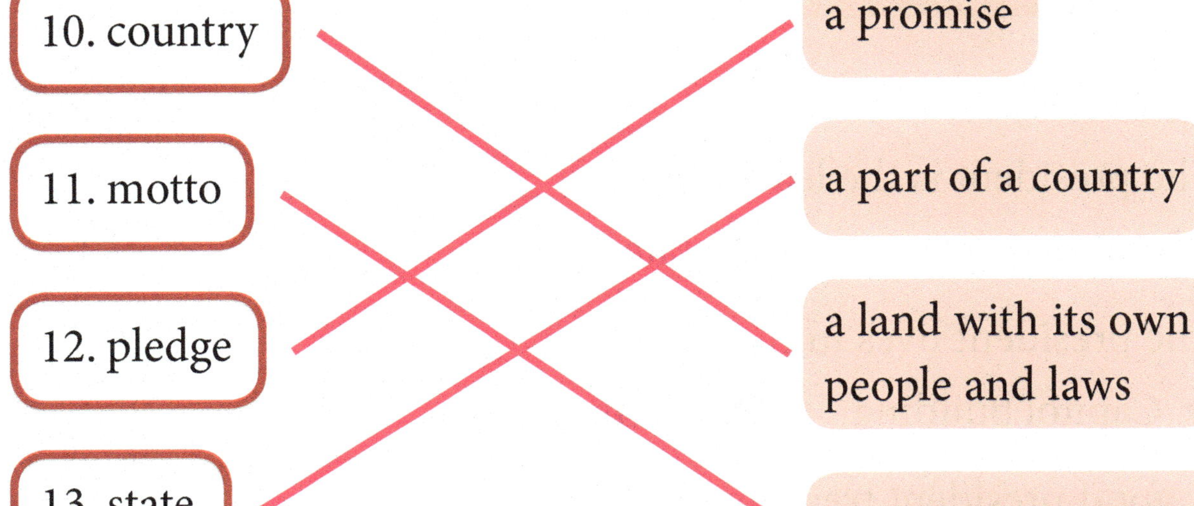

Family and Community

Lesson 68

127

14. 

15. 

16. 

17. 

18. 

19. The president is the leader of the _____.
   ● country   ○ state

20. The president lives in the _____.
   ○ Capitol building   ● White House

21. A good president treats everybody _____.
   ○ differently   ● fairly

Family and Community

Name _______________________

Glue each picture from the next page in the correct box.

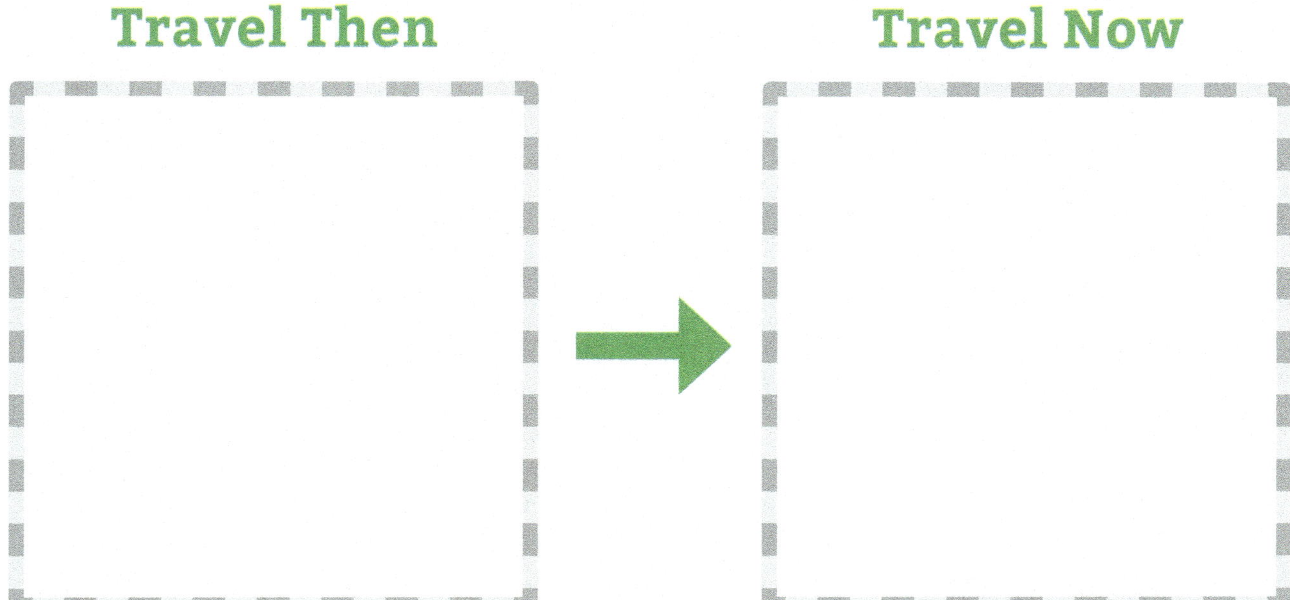

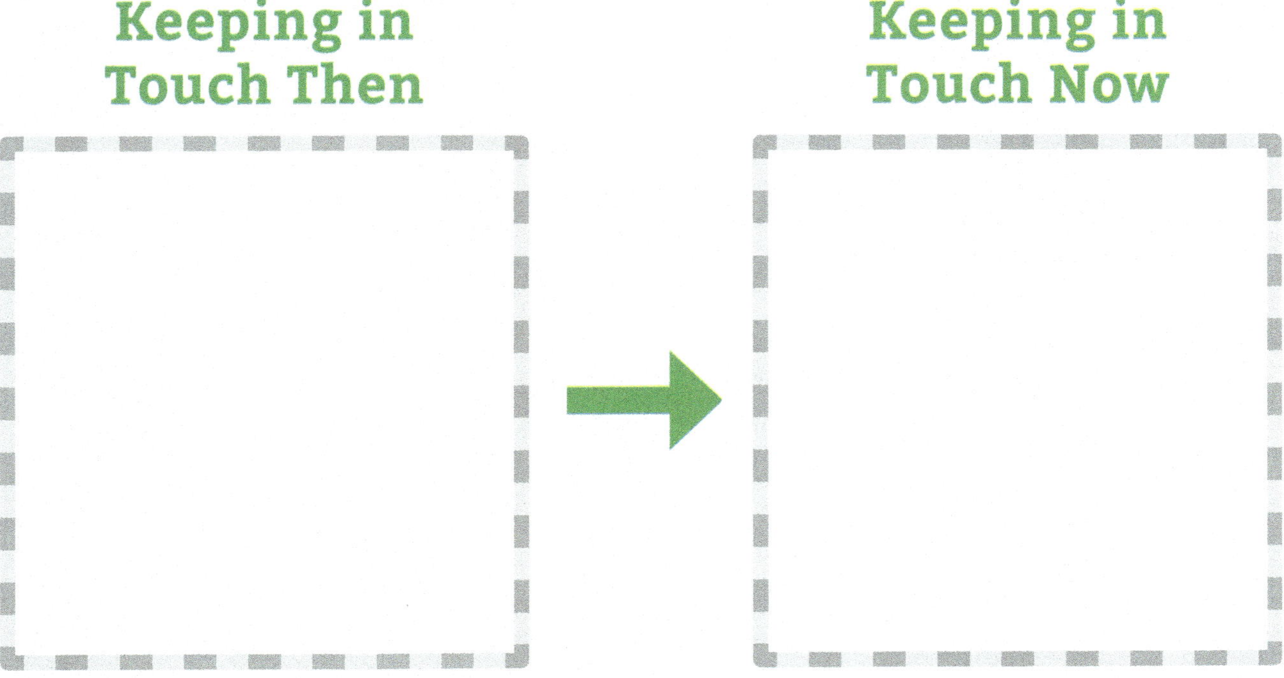

Then and Now: Travel and Keeping in Touch

Cut out the pictures.

Family and Community

Past, Present, and Future

Name _______________________

Past

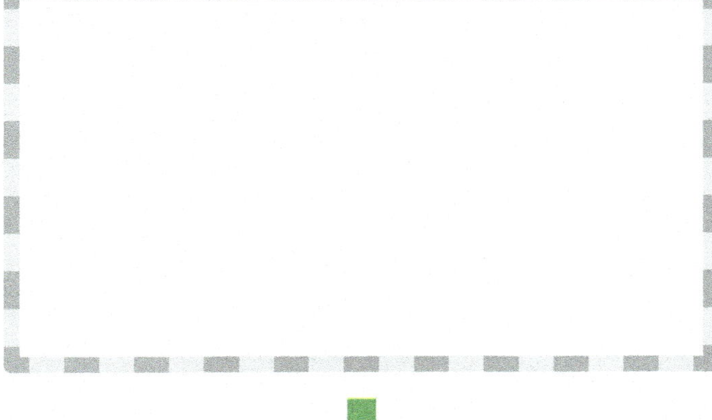

Present

Future

Past, Present, and Future

Family and Community

Sources for Learning About the Past

Circle each picture that shows a way to learn about the past.

1.

2.

3.

4.

5.

6.

Native American Artifacts

Circle each picture that shows an artifact that teaches us about Native Americans.

1. 

2. 

3. 

4. 

5. 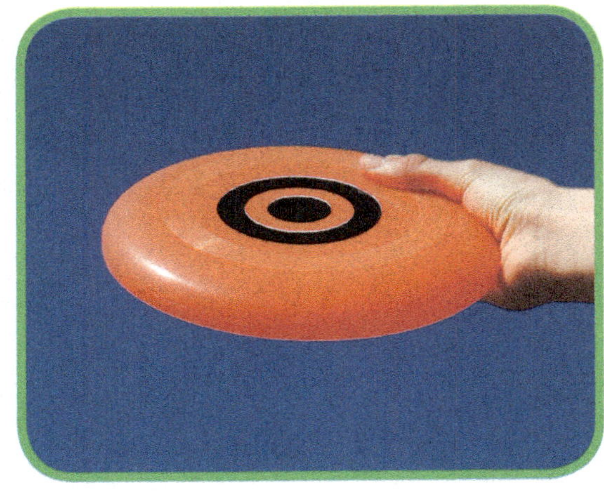

6. 

Voyage to a New World

Write the word or words that complete the sentence.

> **Columbus   explorer   money**
> **New World   voyage**

1. A person who travels to study new places is an _explorer_.

2. _Columbus_ wanted to find a new way to Asia.

3. He would take a long _voyage_ by ship.

4. The king and queen of Spain gave him _money_ for the trip.

5. The voyage reached the _New World_ instead of Asia.

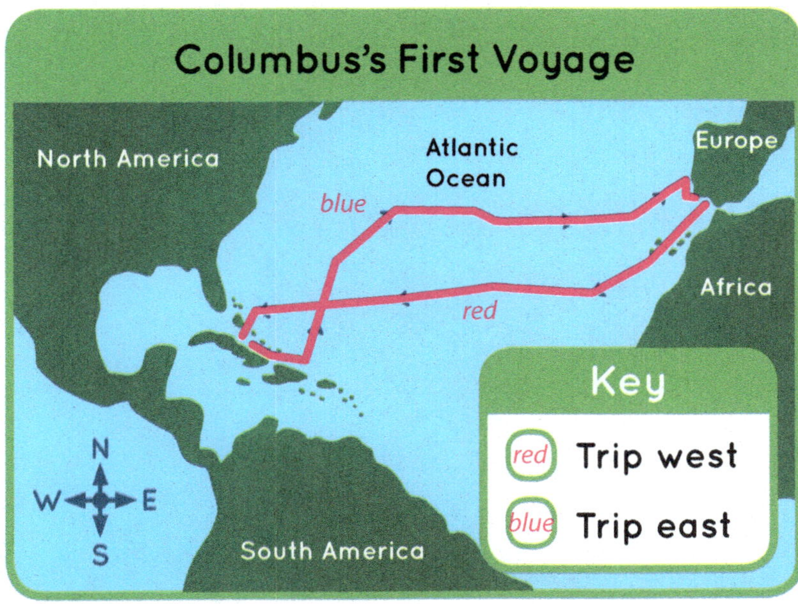

Follow the steps.

1. Use a red crayon to trace the trip west.
2. Use a blue crayon to trace the return trip east.
3. Use a red crayon to color the map key for the trip west.
4. Use a blue crayon to color the map key for the trip east.

Name _______________________

Write **P** if the description is about the Pilgrims.
Write **W** if the description is about the Wampanoag.

____W____ 1. led by a chief

____P____ 2. wrote laws that showed respect to God and the king

____P____ 3. planted vegetables, barley, and wheat

____W____ 4. planted corn, beans, and squash with a fish

____P____ 5. ate vegetables, grain, duck, goose, and wild turkey

____W____ 6. ate bean and squash soup, meat stew, whale, and seal

____W____ 7. wore feathers, jewelry, and deerskin clothes

____P____ 8. wore plain clothes and hats

Important United States Documents

Draw a line from the picture of the document to its name.

1.

2.

Declaration of Independence

Constitution of the United States

Mark the answer.

3. Leaders accepted the _____ on July 4.
   - ○ Constitution of the United States
   - ● Declaration of Independence

4. The document said America was _____.
   - ● free
   - ○ English

5. Later, the leaders signed a new document called the _____.
   - ● Constitution of the United States
   - ○ Declaration of Independence

6. The document had _____ for the new country.
   - ● rules
   - ○ taxes

7. The country chose _____ to be the first president.
   - ○ the king of England
   - ● George Washington

Immigrants' Customs in America

Name ___________________________

1. Draw a line from the place to the custom.

2. Circle the customs that your family takes part in.

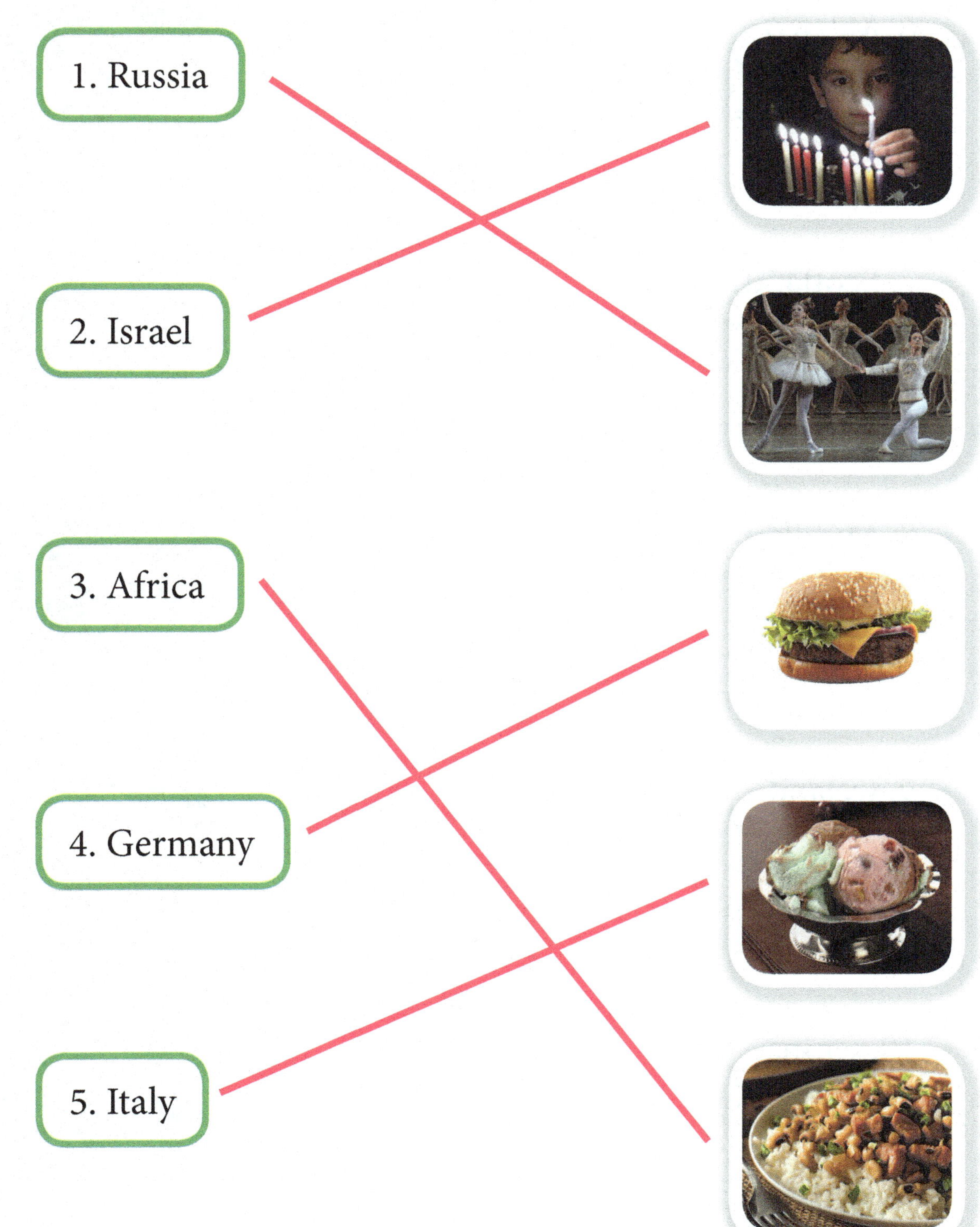

1. Draw a line from the place to the custom.
2. Circle the customs that your family takes part in.

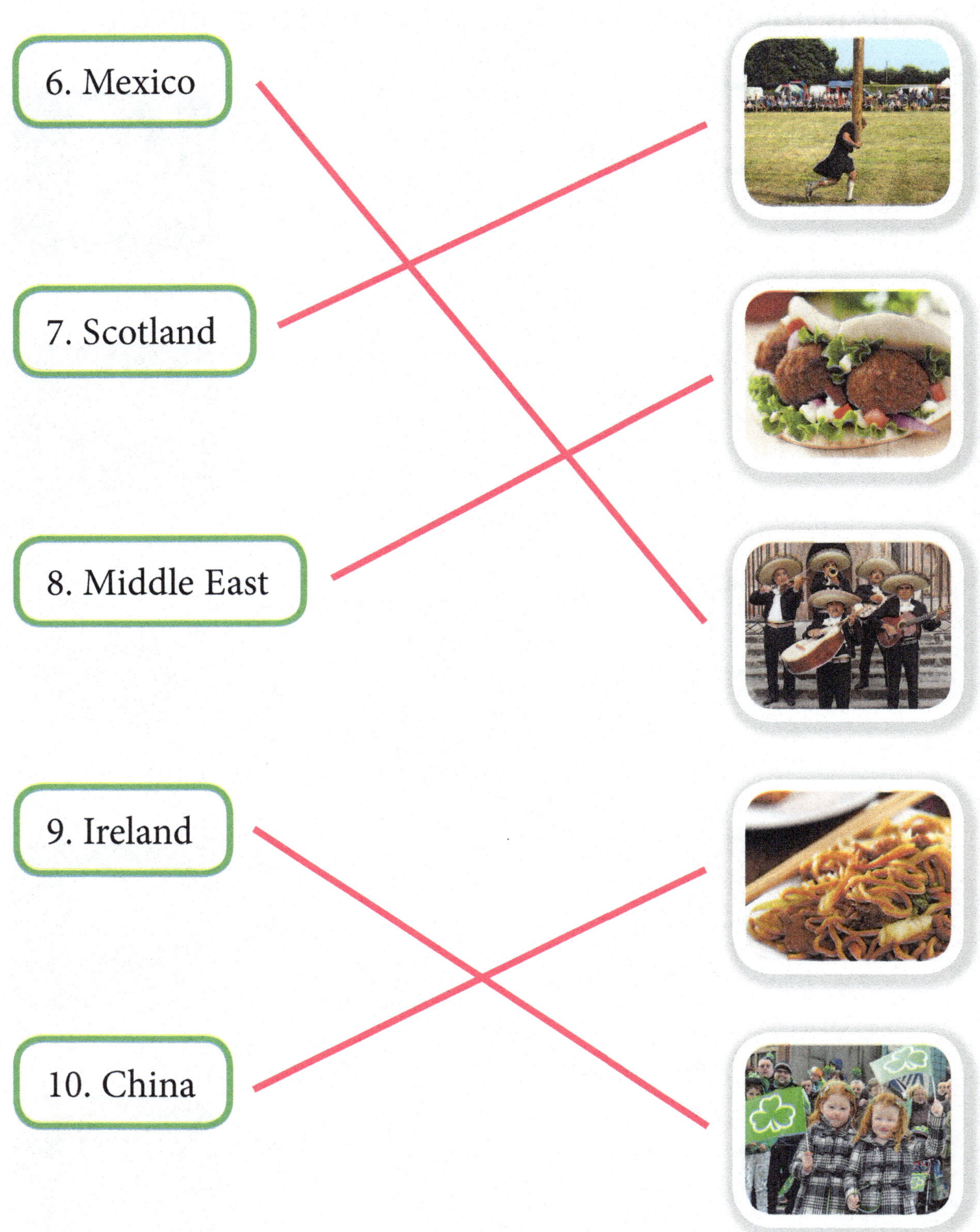

Family and Community

Name _______________________

Draw a modern invention that is used in our country.

Draw one way people keep in touch in our country.

Draw one way people travel in our country.

Timeline: Early History of America

Name _______________________________

Glue the pictures from the next page on the timeline in the order they happened.

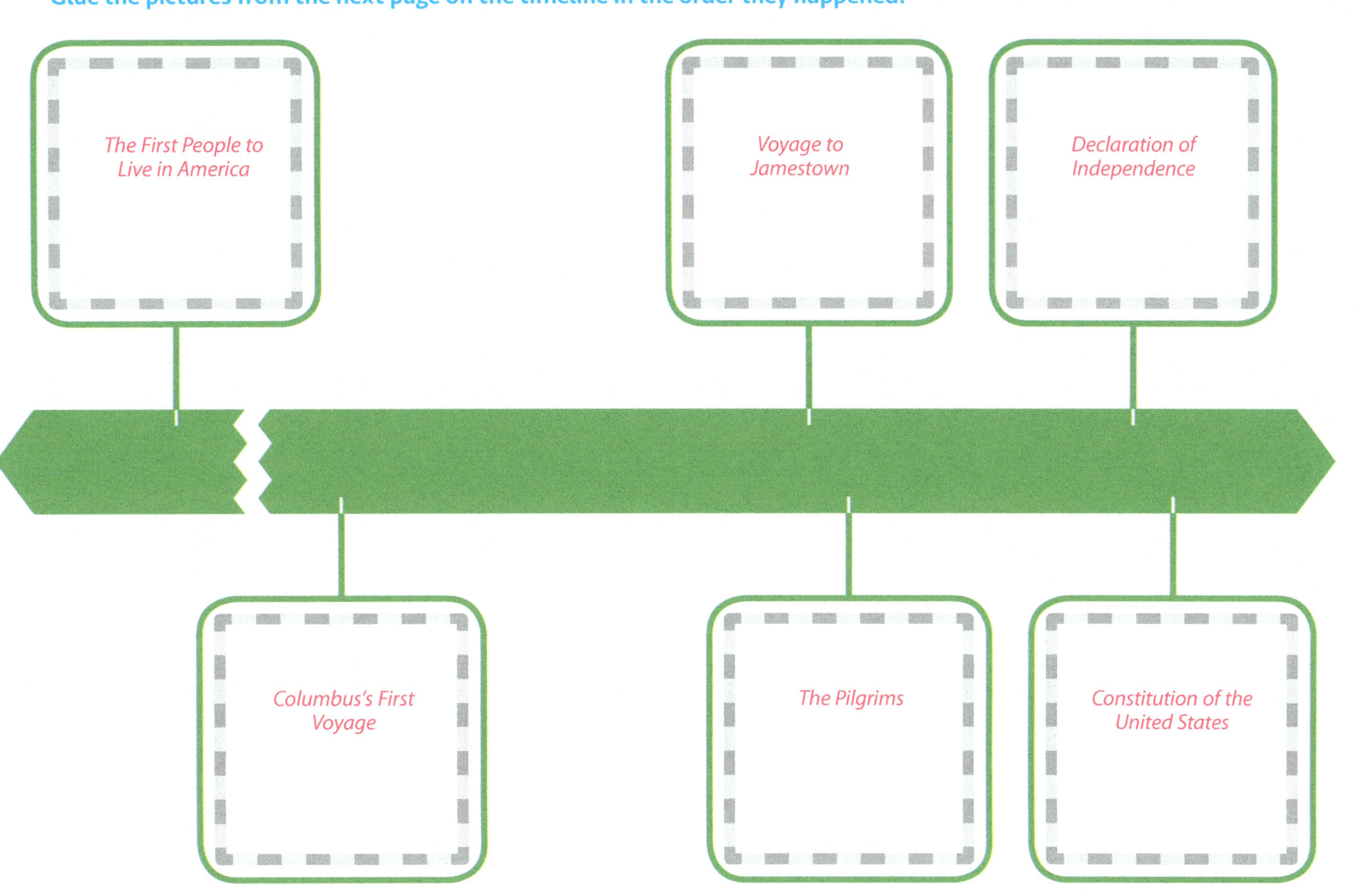

Timeline: Early History of America

Family and Community

Study Guide

Circle the word that completes the sentence.

1. In the past, travel by horse-drawn wagon was _____.   fast   slow

2. In the past, keeping in touch was _____ too.   fast   slow

3. Today, technology helps people travel _____ by airplane.   fast   slow

4. Today, keeping in touch is _____ by phone and computer.   fast   slow

5. A story of the past is called _____.   history   events

Pretend that today is February 14. Draw a line from the question to the answer.

6. What event is today?

7. What event is in the future?

8. What event is in the past?

February

Sun	Mon	Tue	Wed	Thu	Fri	Sat
						1
2 Groundhog Day	3	4	5	6	7	8
9	10	11	12	13	14 Valentine's Day	15
16	17 Presidents' Day	18	19	20	21	22
23	24	25	26	27	28	29

Family and Community

Write the word that completes the sentence.

> **artifacts   Native   primary   secondary**

9. Sources that come from people who were at an event

   are *primary* _______________ sources.

10. Sources that come from people who did not see the event

   are *secondary* _______________ sources.

11. The first people to live in North America after the Flood

   were *Native* _______________ Americans.

12. We study *artifacts* _______________ to learn about the first people in a place.

Mark the answer.

13. _____ sailed west to reach Asia but found new lands instead.
    - ○ The king of Spain
    - ● Christopher Columbus

14. People in England sailed to the new lands hoping to find _____.
    - ○ tribes
    - ● gold and other resources

15. The Pilgrims sailed to America, where they could _____.
    - ● worship God the way the Bible says
    - ○ get rich

16. The Declaration of Independence said Americans were _____.
    - ○ English citizens
    - ● free to have their own country

Name ___________________________

Mark the answer.

17. The Constitution of the United States had _____ for the new country.

    ○ taxes   ● rules

18. _____ became the first president of the United States.

    ○ Chief Massasoit   ● George Washington

19. People who leave their country and move to another one are called _____.

    ● immigrants   ○ natives

20. The people who move to the United States from many different countries bring _____ to our country.

    ● customs   ○ pizzas